cowboy memories of montana

cowboy memories
of montana

Mark Perrault

University of Idaho Press
Moscow, Idaho
1997

Copyright © 1997 The University of Idaho Press
Published by the University of Idaho Press
Moscow, Idaho 83844-1107
Printed in the United States of America
All rights reserved

Typography by WolfPack

01 00 99 98 97   5 4 3 2 1

Library of Congress Cataloging-in-Publication Data

Perrault, Mark, 1915–
   Cowboy memories of Montana
         / Mark Perrault
      p.   cm.
   ISBN 0–89301–207–6 (alk. paper)
   1. Ranch life—Montana—Madison County—History—20th
century. 2. River Ranch (Mont.) 3. Cowboys—Montana—
Madison County—Biography. 4. Madison County (Mont.)—
Social life and customs. 5. Perrault, Mark, 1915–   . I. Title.
F737.M2P47   1997
978.6'663032'092
[B]—DC21   96-51484
                                                              CIP

Magloire Perrault, one of Montana's early pioneers, made a journey of three thousand miles to reach the Missouri head-waters country. His lovely and dutiful wife, their progeny and contemporaries, old-time cowboys with their herds of calico cattle, and farmers scattered here and there, were a driving force in building a new state. The success of these hardy folks and their families was the hot iron that left a permanent brand on the state of Montana. Here is their story. To each of them, and to my father and mother who played such an important part, I dedicate this writing.

contents

illustrations

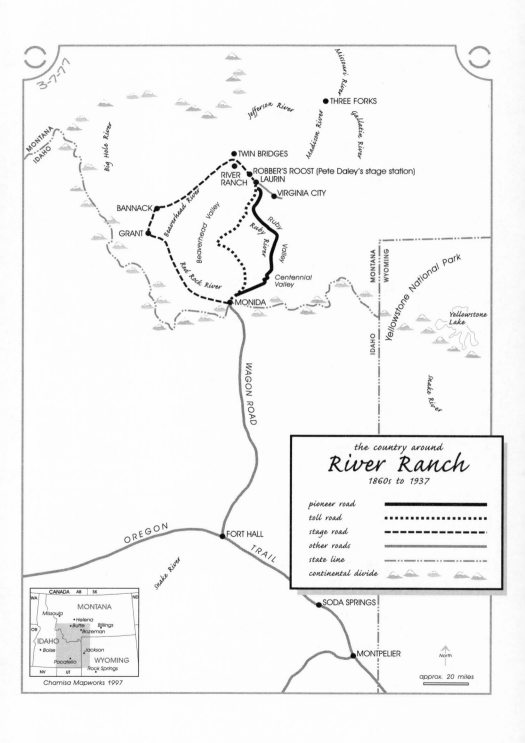

the country around
River Ranch
1860s to 1937

pioneer road	▬▬▬▬▬▬
toll road	■■■■■■■
stage road	▬ ▬ ▬ ▬
other roads	▬▬▬▬▬▬
state line	∙∙∙∙∙∙∙
continental divide	🞂🞂🞂🞂

Chamisa Mapworks 1997

approx. 20 miles

preface

In the mid-1800s, the country bounded by the headwaters of the Missouri River was one of the last unspoiled frontiers in the nation. The Missouri forms at Three Forks where the Jefferson, Madison, and Gallatin Rivers come together, and from there flow eastward to join the Mississippi. If you follow the Jefferson southwest from Three Forks toward the Continental Divide, as did Lewis and Clark in the summer of 1805, the river divides into two tributaries above Twin Bridges—the Ruby, which flows southeast, and the Beaverhead, which flows southwest. In the headwaters of the rivers in the southwestern corner of Montana is a wedge of sacred land that borders Idaho and Wyoming. Within that area lies vast ranges of prairie, mountain valleys, and grassy meadows.

It was in the headwaters of the Missouri River that the improvement of the mixed breeds of early cattle began in earnest. The first calico cattle pulled the westering prarie wagons giving milk along the way. In the early 1800s, only Indians, trappers, and a few explorers had visited or lived in this remote country. The Great Spirit had willed these lands to the Crow, Blackfeet, Nez Percés, Flatheads, and Shoshones. In the narrow Centennial Valley north of the Continental Divide, the many birds and game animals provided rich resources for the Indian tribes. Buffalo were more abundant than on the plains, because the slopes here gently rise northward to a low divide in the Gravelly Range. Beginning on the north slope of that low divide the Ruby River was named Philanthropy by Lewis and Clark. Indians and old-time pioneers called it Pak-Sam-Ma-Oi or Pah-Ma-Mar-Oi. Later it became Stinkingwater, and finally Montana legislature named the river Ruby.

The first cattlemen in this almost vacant land were the Grant brothers, frontiersmen who trailed half-starved cattle that they had

Sheridan, Montana, about 1905

purchased from emigrants along the Oregon Trail over the low mountain pass of the Continental Divide, called Monida Pass. They wintered the stock and let them recover from the 1,000-mile trail. The next year they sold the cattle to other emigrants, trading more exhausted stock for renewed cows on a two-for-one basis. With the discovery of gold at midcentury, people of every stripe invaded this frontier paradise—prospectors, miners, gold camp followers, and businessmen—wanting to acquire any wealth that might be found.

Among the earliest arrivals was a young Frenchman barely past his teens, Magloire Perrault, my grandfather. He was born in 1841 in St. Jaques L'Archigan, Canada, and must have come by the Overland Trail, which had French settlements all along it. From Fort Bridger he likely took the Oregon Trail to old Fort Hall. A trail north, the major north-south transportation corridor into the region, led to the Continental Divide at Monida and thence into the Missouri headwaters. Actual dates and events in his journey have been lost because the Frenchman was unlettered, but it is clear he was among the earliest pioneers of the headwaters country.

Magloire Perrault was not the least bit interested in Montana's gold. As that violent, raucous endeavor whimpered to a close, he saw his future in the fertile land—the valleys, the meadows, and *the trout-filled streams. For a number of years he freighted along the pioneer roads south to Salt Lake City to accumulate the necessary capital so he, too, could buy some half-starved cattle and realize his dream.*

Near the present town of Sheridan, Montana, Grandfather Perrault built a cabin on open range near Mill Creek with a man named Breer. In 1863 the Enabling Act gave most of the land near Sheridan to the Northern Pacific Railroad, and Magloire Perrault found himself a displaced squatter. Moving on was a common frontier experience. But, because of the abundance of vacant land, anyone could find a place to live; although, without paying for a land survey, one could not establish legal ownership of a homestead.

The first recorded transaction naming Magloire Perrault as owner appears in the records of Madison County, Idaho Territory, in 1868 and concerns a tract of land near Laurin, Montana, south of Sheridan. It was a 160-acre parcel, "bounded on the north by Fornier's ranch, east of Combs's ranch, south of Morier's ranch, and west of a 'high mountain' (Ruby Mountain) on the banks of Stinkingwater River in Stinkingwater Township." Three months later he sold it for a profit of $400.

In 1872 Magloire Perrault and James Desdier purchased what would become River Ranch from Sebastian Audifred, who had purchased the land from Pvt. Capt. William Leland or Leland's heirs. On November 3, 1835, Congress had passed an act granting far western land to soldiers as bounty land in payment for military service, and Leland had received one tract, under warrant #10833, as payment for serving in the War of 1812.

The recording of the deed in Madison County, Idaho Territory records brought to life the Frenchman's dream of a cattle ranch. The new ranch stretched along the Ruby River valley and was protected by 10,000-foot peaks: Old Baldy to the east, Table Mountain to the north, Ruby Mountain to the west, and Baldy Mountain, which would become the summer range for cattle, at the north end of the Gravelly Range. Grandfather's cattle brand, two quarter circles became one of the oldest recorded brands in Montana.

After Grandfather and his partner bought the River Ranch, they cut the brush along the river and built ditches with the aid of strong backs, a team of horses, a sulky plow, and untold hours of shovel-handle shining. They fenced the meadows for cows to graze the climax grasses. The original log cabin was built on high ground in a river oxbow. Often in the spring, floodwaters covered the site and hordes of mosquitoes followed. Grandfather Perrault bought out his partner, Breer, and over time continued to add more property to the ranch until in 1911 the ranch covered over a mile of meadowland along both sides of the river, which almost split the ranch in two. Its many oxbows caused the length of the river to be more than twice the length of the land it flowed through.

The cattle ranching days of Grandfather Perrault crisscross some of the most memorable dates, lands, and events in early Montana history. He rode the old stage road from Pete Daley's station (now Robber's Roost) across the corner of the ranch through rattlesnake and grasshopper country north of the Ruby mountains into the Beaverhead Valley. He followed the toll road from Daley's station across Sweetwater country to Monida Pass. The pioneer road upon which he trailed his cows was a wagon track east of Ruby River to the Gravelly Range and into Centennial Valley. He shared the stage stations and saloons in the region with the famous and infamous. And through turbulent and changing times, he cared for his cows, carried no gun, and was rewarded by becoming a successful rancher.

One day when Grandfather went to the village of Laurin to visit relatives and friends from Canada, he met Pamela Le Gris, my grandmother. She had crossed the plains from Illinois, by routes unknown when she was ten years old, to live with her sister Adeline and Adeline's husband, J. B. Laurin. My grandmother's eyes would twinkle and her lined and weathered face would light up when she recounted her first meeting with that young Frenchman. According to French custom, she said, the goodbyes were always accompanied with a kiss of farewell. With that farewell kiss, Grandmother knew she must marry Magloire Perrault—and she did, on May 10, 1881, in the old Catholic church in Laurin with Father Kelleher officiating. Magloire was forty and Pamela was a beautiful young lady of twenty-one. She added pretty curtains to the rude log cabin, as well as the pleasant odor of fine and fancy cooking. They had a son, Frank, my father, who followed in his father's footsteps and continued to improve River Ranch. In time Grandfather and my father developed their scrawny and raw-boned emigrant calico cattle into a fine white-faced Hereford herd.

I grew up on River Ranch with a fishing pole in one hand, a shotgun in the other, and a string of traps over my shoulder. My

childhood memories are of prickly pear cactus peeled and sprin-
kled with salt. Served that way, it was imagined as a sort of deli-
cacy. Prickly pears fixed with salt were memorable, but a sled
tipping over in the cactus patches in winter is hard to forget, too.
And then there was Grandmother, still a beautiful lady even when
I was a child, her face square and full-fleshed, her eyes blue like
the sky and always a-twinkle, her full-breasted, five-foot-two figure
the envy of many ladies. Her hair had gone gray and thin when I
knew her, but it was always neatly combed in a little ball and held
with a ribbon and pin in the back.

I still recall the giant cartwheel cookies from her kitchen, which
I was given on my childhood visits. One corner of the log cabin
was cluttered with pioneer utensils usually found on a prairie
schooner—a candle mold, a bullet mold, an oil lamp—but the one
thing that could not be found was a gold pan. My grandfather's
saddle in the loft is testament, instead, to his life's ambition. It has
seen many miles of meadow, prairie, and mountain, and lots of
rain and storms. The horn has been re-covered many times after a
hard-twist rope burned through the leather to the steel core. Swells
on modern saddles help to hold a cowboy up there, but they are not
found on Grandfather's saddle. The seat is deep and high and it
makes you sit up straight. The sheepskin skirt has only a few tufts
of wool remaining here and there along the edges. The oak stir-
rups, with two-inch-thick soles are worn thin, and the leather on
the saddle is worn through in several places.

In the morning darkness, on a ridge west of River Ranch
that overlooked the meandering river and the ranch below, I
sat on Smoke, my favorite horse, thinking about the old days.
Clad in my warm mackinaw, I could have sat there all day,
dreaming and reliving the events and happenings of the frontier ranch, but today the real world was a thirty- or forty-mile
ride among the white-faced cattle who were my charges. This
was not the same West—it was a different world from the one
Grandfather knew. In his day this range bloomed in spring,
and the climax grasses reached his stirrups and almost
brushed the belly of his horse. In many places deer and antelope traveled unseen through the high grass. In those days
Grandfather might have looked down on a tiny fawn, a buffalo
calf, or an antelope that had no fear of the hunter's gun. The
large animals were joined by jackrabbits, gophers, badgers,

and the many birds of the prairie. These days the same climax grasses reach only to Smoke's knees. The grass still gives sustenance to prairie residents, but it is far from stirrup-high.

As the valley became settled and its meadows fenced, the Gravelly Range came to be used for summer pasture. Cattle ranching became a two-season, two-area endeavor. Most of River Ranch was still made up of the wild meadows originally found in the valley. The grass was especially prominent where the water table was high and the soil damp. Above the meadows, irrigated land came to be farmed with introduced crops like alfalfa, clover, and grain. The native grasses and introduced crops in the valley fields were harvested for winter livestock forage. In the mountain ranges the high grama and fescue climax grasses were the best in summer and produced the fattest cattle, and the high country was free range. It was only necessary to drive the stock there in spring, spend minimal time caring for them in summer, and bring them home in fall.

The free mountain ranges, combined with valley hayfields made it possible to run many more cattle, and a provident and astute rancher could increase his herd size ten times at no further cost. A 640-acre section of meadow, or meadow and alfalfa land, would take care of winter forage for up to five hundred head of cattle.

Free summer range for the same cattle required five or six thousand acres of grassland. The ranchers had no problem pooling their herds in the spring and then splitting them again in the fall; this was the beginning of the trail drives of common herds of cattle in the headwaters region.

In the days before the Great War, the cattle in the headwaters region were much like those with which Grandfather had started his ranching days. They were mostly shorthorn and mixed breeds—just cattle. Nelson Story was the first to trail Texas cattle over the Bozeman Trail into Montana. He was followed by others, like Joe Redfern of the Judith Basin. But the only success of the longhorns in the headwaters were a few aged steers still around in Father's time, which had stampeded and taken up residence in the brush and swamps of the Centennial Valley.

Shortly after the turn of the century, Father, before his first score of years, caused a change in the open range of the

Gravelly when he brought in a Hereford bull from Denver. That summer of the first white-faced Hereford was unique. The bull proved to be a fighter of prodigious talent and a breeder of great strength. When the next spring came and calves began to drop, the value of that Hereford bull was clear to see. Before spring trail began, the reputation of that bull and of my father were secure. Thereafter, Hereford bulls were the only bulls allowed on the open ranges of the Gravellys; bulls of other breeds were banned, and selective breeding began on the open range. Hit-and-miss breeding by lazy old shorthorn bulls, or just any old bull who often hid out in the mountain swamps, was about to change. Calving still took place throughout the year, but dry cows became rare. Other improvements followed, and today several breeds of beef cattle have been developed. Herefords are still a prominent breed, but the open range where they first roamed has passed into history, wrapped in barbed wire.

This is the story of the cattle and the men who cared for and loved them. It is the story of that Smoke horse, whose lineage can be traced back to Nez Percé breeders. And it is the story of white-faced Hereford cattle and the outdoors in which they lived. Much has been written about the gold miners, road agents, and vigilantes of Montana's early history. This story concerns the pioneers who chose to toil on the land, whose names are not often recalled. The solid pioneers, like Magloire Perrault, his family, and his descendants, remain the mainstay of places like the Ruby Valley throughout Montana. These are memories of my life there as I was growing up. River Ranch was not only a ranch—for me it was a legend, with its oxbows, groves of willows, birch, and wild rosebushes, its birds and animals, and its meadows that flowed into the endless prairies of the truly great open spaces of Montana. It is now a memory in the history of the West, and this is its story.

introduction

River Ranch, a Montana cattle ranch on the Ruby River had spanned three quarters of a century when the years finally rolled around to the 1930s. Each of those years was almost a replay of the earliest one on the ranch.

A new era of cattle ranching was about to begin. Depression ranching caused rapid change and the entry of modern new methods. Even the cattle began to change with new and better breeds. Some of the earliest players, truly the most colorful, were lost. Indians, the old Indian chief and his small band of Bannock, the explorers and the trappers, my grandfather and many old-timers were gone. Ed Davis, with his barrel-stave legs and Joe Redfern, premier horseman and cattle cowboy, were in the twilight of their lives, nearly the sole survivors of those bygone days of the West and the frontier. My father was no longer a young man.

Buffalo, the symbol of frontier prairies, are nowhere to be found. The stagecoach no longer races its way across the prairie with the six-span, the skinner and his partner riding shotgun with a coach full of frontier people and a strongbox full of gold. Ruts across the fields and the prairie made by the coach will last another century as a reminder of lost frontier days.

Road agents and gunmen are now silent and only the crude wooden markers on Boot Hill record their span. Pete Daley's stage station, now called Robber's Roost, is vacant and almost forgotten. The trail through Centennial Valley and across the Continental Divide, which opened up the last frontier and the sacred land of the Indian, is a trail no longer. Model T's would navigate that trail as a country road in good weather as soon as they were invented.

The old tobacco tins with the criss crossed bales are no longer found. Schools kids must be careful of the ones they have inherited or they'll have to buy one of the newfangled ones, not near so good, for lunches. We can still find a smoker to get the flat tin cans for fishing bait. Shotgun shells cost twenty-five cents more, but that does not guarantee any more ducks.

Big Four tractors are belching and backfiring their last. New tractors and new machines are the talk of all the farmers. How little gasoline the new tractor takes compared to how much hay horses would eat is a debate no one can articulate. Nowadays some wagons are around with rubber tires, there will be no more screeching old iron tires on frozen snow during winter feedings. How will a cow know when she is hungry or where the hay will be dumped off the wagon? No one dared to say how you fixed a flat when it was forty below. I am sure mother would put up with a newborn calf, in a storm, a lot quicker than she would with a wagon wheel in front of that beautiful Home Comfort kitchen stove.

Surreys, with the fringe on top, are collectors' items. Not many of the present farmers or ranchers know what a three-and-a-quarter inch Studebaker wagon is. Soon there will be very few who will know what a neck yoke or a singletree is either.

Rumors were everywhere that the Model T might soon be available in colors other than black. And that new automobiles might have a gadget called a self-starter. No more broken arms, no more runaways with the team hooked onto that old flivver at forty below as it skidded along the snow before belching and firing into life in the winter. Other cars, bigger and more beautiful, would soon be available according to salesmen around the valley.

Electric light plants (32-volt generators) and other new gadgets could be purchased from the "Monkey Ward" catalog (Montgomery Ward was known as Monkey Ward in those days). These new items both made life easier and more pleasureable, and helped farm and ranch life seem less remote. And those catalogs were almost twice as large as the old ones, they just might last all winter.

Ranch life was clearly headed for some great changes and soon. Yet, cows were still going to be cows and they would have fine calves. Thanks to Father our cows were white-faced Herefords. We had the best of these fine cattle in this valley. We rode the best horses and had the best teams of horses. The river still flowed full, and the creek would still clear in summer and be full of trout. The meadows will green, and hay crops will be heavy. The prairie is still free of barbed wire most everywhere. We could still run horses for thirty miles and not have to stop to open a gate. Those nesters were gone and the busted sod acres were showing signs of growing back to the climax grasses. The great summer ranges are still high, wide, and handsome. The sun rises every morning over Old Baldy Mountain and the sky is always clear.

Indeed, ranch life has changed and will change some more, but the bond between the animals and the ranch folks who live among them cannot be broken. Each, the people and the animals, are dependent upon the other. The great outdoors cannot exist without people who live together and respect and understand each other and all Nature's creatures. Determined are we to hold to this wonderful ranch life, in memory of those who made it possible. There will always be a new year, and another year, and each will be better than the year just past.

The sun is bright, the sky is clear, the air is fresh and sharp. It is spring again.

part 1
CATTLE DRIVE

a view from the ridge

It was cold and dark, still an hour before sunrise on the ridge. Smoke, the Appaloosa with one white eye, was tense. His ears were stiff and pointed straight ahead. The horse and I were almost one. It was spring, and the plains for miles around held Nature's gifts and creatures. After a while a halo of light began to show in the east on the crest of Old Baldy Mountain. In no time the cold, dark landscape would be a beehive of activity.

Sitting on Smoke, I watched the huge and purposeful Hereford bulls out on the prairie. They seemed to barely notice us. Their deep-set eyes paid no attention to me or the Appaloosa. Their casual indifference hid a sharp-eyed vigilance and concern for the safety of their charges; the cows moved about to get next to their calves. They would protect those offspring. As they watched us they shook their heads, though their horns had long ago been cut off.

On that prairie back in the 1920s Smoke and I were the West, which few folks today had the privilege of knowing—the huge bulls, the white-faced cows, and their calves. Smoke and I were together on this great plain that was truly the last of the frontier.

As I looked back, there were flickers of other ranchers' lamps. It was very quiet on the crest. The air was sharp, the sky still sparkling with a million fading stars. That plain or prairie above the ranch was the fall and spring range for all the cattle of the valley. It would be a month or so before the cattle now out on it would be gathered and moved to summer range. As yet it had no fence, no barbed wire, to spoil the view.

It was light enough now to see beyond a group of cows guarding a score of calves and find that we have missed the miracle of birth by only a few moments—a newborn calf rises on unsteady legs. The nighthawk swoops close overhead on its last glide over the prairie until evening. Now Smoke and I head farther west.

When it was full day, we made a loop around the prairie on our way back to the ranch. We moved the strays into the herd, checked the heifers that were soon to calve, and rode the edge of the Ruby Mountains. We made certain that the newborn calves had watchful mothers. Save an odd accident, these offspring of half-wild cows were safe from most anything except man. Wolves had been almost erased from Montana many years ago, although once in a while we found a steer with a short tail—the wolf's trademark.

It was time to take a break, walk a ways, and shed the warm mackinaw. The prairie dog town was a carnival. A few old dogs were on guard and most of a million little offspring were scampering about. Two or three golden eagles high in the sky put a stop to the prairie dog show. A couple of squeaks and the scene was so quiet and still it seemed like the night just past.

Two restless cows were guarding a score of small calves. Anyone with twenty kids would be restless, too. The cows turned with every step we took, while the calves were only curious. In the distance a line of cows came up the draw to join, and then relieve, the cows on guard. The guards could now take their turn to water.

This water hole, with its small patch of gravel and no grass, was a sort of accident out there on the sandy plain. Killdeer raced around on toothpick legs, dressed in black neckties and gave sharp chirps. The curlew was another misfit with its great long beak. Both the killdeer and curlew ran about screaming with broken wings, which weren't really broken but rather a way to distract us from their nests. Smoke knew that act well. All range horses and cow horses would change their path if possible to avoid these broken wings. Both nests, one with speckled jelly beans and the other with one egg like a turkey egg, were easily found from the back of a horse, but to a man walking along at ground level, these nests were almost impossible to see.

We were close to Sand Hollow, a gash across the middle of the prairie ten miles long and maybe a hundred feet deep and a hundred yards wide. Its sandstone and limestone ledges were home to many plains creatures, including rattlesnakes. Swallows were flying everywhere, busy with their adobe nests on the edges of the limestone outcrops. As we eased along the rim we could see a pair of coyotes. Their den was a couple of hundred yards away. It was easy to find the bones of rabbits and other small animals near where we were; closer to the den, the bones had been carried away. Seldom did we see the coyote pups; one yelp from the old coyotes and those pups would disappear. Directly beneath us, below the rim, was a rattlesnake den. In spring the rattlesnakes had left the den and were scattered widely, but next fall we will be much more careful here.

We were halfway across our range and across Sand Hollow, and had to hurry to the west bench edge to gather and push strays to better grass.

Stage wheel tracks were still almost a foot deep where they cross the prairie and enter the Beaverhead Valley, headed on to the Grasshopper and Bannock diggings. The tracks bent here and there to miss some wash or bar. I looked back and closed my eyes and could see a six-span Concord stage coming over the rise. The driver, lines and whip in hand, and the shotgun rider, were on the driver's seat. This stage came from Virginia City, past Nevada City, past Adobe Town and Pete Daley's stage station, across a corner of the ranch, then over the Stinkingwater River, up the slope, and over the buffalo jump to the open prairie. When I opened my eyes the dream faded away in the dust of the coach wheels.

It is peaceful here with cattle scattered over the many miles of climax grass. We tried to keep them in a sort of scattered herd. There was a band of wild horses on their way to water at the edge of the prairie. Smoke came from a band like that, wild and carefree. A tension in his muscles and twitching in his ears were sure proof that he had not forgotten. I was a bit more careful. It was a long way back to the ranch on foot, and these high-heeled boots did not walk worth a damn.

At the western edge of the prairie, silent monuments of metal stood in the open before us, rusting away beneath sun and storms, a testimony to the failure of man. These once usable farm machines now stood mute. There was a Big Four tractor with wheels as high as my horse and a threshing machine never used, along with other farm equipment. Here

hundreds of acres of virgin prairie climax grass had been
plowed up and sometimes planted to crops that did not bloom,
grow, or ripen. On the edge of Sand Hollow stood a two-story
house that I had visited. It was no longer a home, yet there
were still dishes on the table and clothes in the closets. It is a
house, silent and deserted, no life, no children, only the scampering of rats and mice. In the yard there are gopher mounds
and badger holes, and runways criss crossed the stone founda-
tion. A few cliff swallows built mud nests on the porch wall
next to the ceiling. A rusted, long-handled pump stood a few
feet from the kitchen door, with a clump of rhubarb growing
close by. I had often taken the tender shoots home for pie
wondering how, without a home, it could still grow.

From the front door of that lonesome, deserted house, looking west was a sad and depressing sight. Most of these hundreds of acres of busted sod were still barren and desolate,
with little or no plant life. Wind-banked sand dunes leaned
against the long-dead furrows. This was a land of busted sod
and broken dreams. It would be years before this man-made
wasteland would be prairie again, but Nature would take it
back and the climax grass would someday be home to the
birds and animals who once lived here. Surely then man will
have seen the folly of his ways and will give pause before cre-
ating a wasted land like that before me.

 Smoke and I turned north and pushed a young bull and a
small herd of cattle east to the main grazing herd. They would
find some company there and be away from this busted sod,
where grass was now a dream that broke my heart.

When the sun was high, the air was still clear and sharp.
The sheen of color against the sun's rays was prairie green.
Some of the grass was tall stalks, though the bases were often
a shear of toothpick-green spines. The rosettes hugging the
ground on small plants would be Montana bitterroot in a few
short days. Soon, too, there would be many more prairie flowers of every color. Most would be next to Mother Earth, but
some would bloom two feet high with long stalks to hold the
flowers. Many of the blooms would be in colors and shades so
delicate they could not be described.

There would be purple lupine and cream-colored locoweed,
a favorite of our old mare Kate. She was goofy when she was

on the weed—drug addiction in the raw. There would be the beautiful larkspur, which grew on the high slopes where the cattle seldom went that time of year. There in patches on the sandy plain were prickly pear cactus, which would be in full bloom soon, with delicate yellow and red flowers. Among the prickly pear were tall blazing stars with gray-green stalks, thin fuzzy leaves, and fragile yellow blooms that opened only at night. They did not smell nearly as good as they looked, yet bumblebees were often seen on these meadow flowers. The beautiful flowers fade away in the fall, which is when the oil in the plant was used as one of the Indians' staple foods.

The sun was now high, almost directly overhead. Such a day is hard to come by in the spring in Montana. The wild horses were just now coming back from water. The stud in the lead was a hundred yards ahead, his head high, his mane aflare, and his tail streaming out most of five feet when he ran. The stud's ears looked like two small spikes in his unkempt forelock. He was a bay whose lineage could not be guessed. Wild mares, yearlings, and colts, some colts only a few days old, kept pace as though on a racetrack. The watchful eyes of the mothers never left them. Great mats of hair, warm winter blankets, hung from the sides of the mothers. Manes were long and some of their tails dragged on the ground. We would see them again close up because we'd need some of them—the largest and strongest—for haying on the ranch.

I had watched the wild studs battle for control of the herd—the most brutal combat one could imagine. One stud would try, and sometimes succeed, to maim the other or drive him away. Their screams could be heard for miles. Often they were bloodied and battered from bite marks. When one unlucky mustang fell, he was kicked again and again. The wild studs would continue to fight until one or the other was subdued. The loser limped away with his head down in a pitiful manner. Often he was so beaten and exhausted that he died from his wounds or the exertion.

A pair of golden eagles drifted high overhead and a flock of crows held a meeting around an old mining claim. Some greenhorn prospector must have thought that this lonesome gravel bar out on the treeless plain was hiding gold. What he did not know was that gold on the prairie was green gold—grass. The price of that bounty was throwing away the gold pan and pick, and getting a horse, a pair of chaps, and some cows, just as my grandfather and father did.

Cattle were scattered as far as the eye could see. Cows and calves were mostly mothered up. Some mothers were busy grazing, some busy—as mothers always are—with the task of shining up their offspring.

It was long past noon and the sun's rays outlined the sharp scarp of Beaverhead Rock, the name Lewis and Clark gave this Shoshone landmark when they passed it more than a century ago. Those explorers would see a changed landscape today. Coyotes still sang music in the mornings, but their heads did not show as they bobbed along the prairie. Nowadays most coyotes are found next to ravines and in the gullies and scattered sage, for that is where their prey lives. Elk and deer had retreated to the mountains or river bottoms. Buffalo, those magnificent beasts, had been replaced by cows.

But rattlesnakes were as plentiful near Beaverhead Rock as they had ever been. Snakes' food consists mainly of bugs: beetles and grasshoppers, which are plentiful on the prairie. Prairie country is rattlesnake country, and there are several species, each with a separate territory. There are the slow, shrinking violets in yellows and greens, stretching several feet, and as big around as your arm, with fangs most of an inch long. They gain respect from their size and rattlesnake reputation, yet they are the least dangerous. The black fellows—rarely more than two and a half feet long—won't run, but neither will they choose to pick a fight. You have to give them the right of way or find some rocks or a stick. But the little gray monsters are plain dangerous. They're feisty as a little dog, and they can kill you and be happy about it.

When Grandfather Perrault began to buy land to put the ranch together, he put the buildings in a central location, near the bench and away from the flooding meadow and the great cottonwood trees. The gravel fan a mile or so south of the ranch buildings was the home of the Water Hole Clan of Rattlesnakes. This fan had a lot of prickly pear and scraggly sage and dozens of gophers. The big green-and-yellow snakes made a home here. We often watched those big snakes stalk the gophers. They would lie coiled, ready to strike, next to the mounds of gopher holes. When the unsuspecting gopher appeared, lightning struck. The now helpless gopher was mostly paralyzed and could not pull away from the long fangs. The snake would lie stretched out and swallow that squealing gopher, who clawed the dirt as it disappeared into the snake. In the fall, the rattlesnakes retired to a den near the old buffalo jump or in the Big Hollow.

The Old House Clan of Rattlesnakes was found on a cactus-and-sage-covered gravel fan that stretched before one of the old homestead cabins north of the ranch buildings. These snakes were generally of the black and gray variety. The gravel fan petered out at a canyon head with limestone caves and small holes and crevices. We all gave this canyon a wide berth in the summer, and especially in the fall when the snakes denned up.

Our ranch house and other buildings sat between these two gravel fans, and the yard was the meeting place for the two rattlesnake clans. Fortunately, rattlers did not like people, or even big animals, and they chose a solitary and passive lifestyle, especially in the warm summertime. When it was cold, and especially if it was wet and cold, rattlesnakes hide if possible because they become almost immobile until the sun warms them.

One day as I headed out to the prairie, I rode past the orchard and tried a couple of green apples. Well, by the time I got to the prairie, those apples had taken over. With a king-sized bellyache, I made for the only sagebrush in sight. After almost falling off my horse and then down on my hands and knees, I began to crawl for the shade of that sagebrush. Suddenly there I was, not much more than a foot or so off the ground, looking squarely into the face of a big old yellow rattler. He was so surprised, it was a second or two before he rattled. He had the shade first, and it was clear as he coiled up that he was going to keep it. It was amazing how the sight of that snake cured my bellyache. I got back up on my horse and headed out to the prairie.

Some horses cannot be trusted and cannot be used where rattlesnakes are found. We had a favorite mare who would buck until you came off whenever she saw or heard one. If that failed, she would lie down and roll on you. That mare stayed home and got fat.

Most cattle and horses will race away from the sound of the rattlesnake, some then get curious and return to investigate. When a snake strikes an animal in the face it generally causes the loss of one eye and sometimes the loss of most of the hair. A cow with a pink hide and no hair is not a common sight in Montana, and she is a real problem in winter.

When sheep were introduced to Montana, the prairies were a natural environment for them. When a ewe had a lamb, the herder would catch her with a hook like David used in biblical days. He would place the ewe and her newborn lamb in a little tent. The tent prevented the ewe from leaving her lamb and it also kept coyotes from having a tasty dinner. Lambing was under way now, and there were a great many little tents on the north end of the prairies. At night the lanterns in them looked almost like stars close to the ground.

We checked all the cattle, made the turn, and headed back to the ranch. Soon we were standing on the rim where we sat in the dark that morning. Now at dusk the light dimmed and the nighthawks began their glides over the prairie. Old Baldy Mountain would catch the last rays of the sun, which would soon fade from view; then the mountain's crest of snow would be outlined with the stars of the western sky. The day was soon a western night. We started on the few short miles to the ranch, me thinking about supper and Smoke thinking about oats.

spring roundup

I was with the lead, a few cattle led by the old steer with the raggedy tail. Big Hollow and the flats on either side held scattered groups of cattle for miles around. In a short while I turned the lead from Big Hollow into the lane. Spring range time was almost past, and we were taking the cattle into the fields. Soon we would be branding and docking the calves, and in another week or so we'd head up the trail, traveling close to a hundred miles, into the summer pasture in the mountains. The lowing of the cows and the bawling of the calves was western music in such a herd. The noise had meaning understood by all those cattle and by the cowboys, too.

The old steer was far past his prime. He was kept and cared for because he was the leader, both on the prairie and on the trail to summer range. He was quite a steer in many ways. His face had three red spots, while almost none of the other cattle had a mark to mar their white faces. The steer was taller by half a foot than the cows he led. His horns had been cut off years ago, but he had other interesting features. His left side had a long scar, a range souvenir, and his tail was short by almost a foot, the end missing the usual tassel of hair. The tail was really just a piece of hide a few inches long tied to a crooked framework of bone. The wolf who had chased this old steer did not get a full meal, but I bet he got a real run. Now the old steer was way ahead, inspecting everything and rarely looking back. The lane was full of cattle, and in a short mile they would be running into the pasture.

In the distance down the lane I saw Ed Davis, a legendary horseman, leading old blood-red Joe, his horse. Joe was saddled up, complete with a slicker tied on behind the saddle and a rope coiled next to the saddle horn, ready to go. Ed never stood six feet tall, probably more like five foot eight or a little less. Now bent over with a hobble gait, Ed could not have been much more than five feet. Those lean hips and once-broad shoulders seemed to fit in with the bronc-riding legends that were spun about Ed Davis. His riding feats on wild horses and his ability with wild broncos were always a source of wonderment to all the ranchers, particularly the younger folks. Horses, or at least the wildest ones, those that could buck the hardest, were always associated with Ed Davis, Joe Redfern, and Frank Perrault.

Years ago Ed's hat must have been the pride and joy of J. B. Stetson, but it had died a while back and somehow had not gone to heaven. One glance would convince most anyone that that hat had indeed been through hell. This would be understandable, for in the days of Ed's exploits, the valley had many times been compared to hell. The front brim of Ed's hat was held fast with a fancy pin. The left side drooped in discouragement. The crown was creased with holes and slices. Scant protection from the Montana weather was afforded by Ed's hat, which was more or less held together with a leather band far too narrow to conceal the sweat of western summers or the frost of western winters.

The face beneath the brim was wide of forehead and framed with wisps of sand-colored hair, which was almost without gray streaks. Ed's clear blue eyes, set deep in their sockets and lined with wrinkles on the edges, were sharp and missed nothing. They were the legacy of western sun and storm and years of searching the western horizon. Ed's cheeks were splotched with red and his nose was striped in red and white—many times frozen, many times sunburned. Ed's right ear was not much of an ear, but it was still tied to his head. The edge of that ear was bright red as though frozen, even though it was shirt-sleeve weather. I suspected that the ear had gotten the worst of it when Ed rode in those bitter cold blizzards.

As I watched Ed come to meet me, I realized that he did not walk at all. His legs seemed not to track like legs were supposed to. His left leg ended in a high-heeled boot that had to turn sharply to meet the ground squarely. No question—that leg would fit a horse almost perfectly. His right leg made one feel that a barrel stave had somehow been saved from the woodpile. Also bowed, that leg is somehow tied to his body at one end and stuck into a high-heeled boot at the other.

Ed Davis and his horse, Joe, were now close by. I dropped off my horse and took the reins in hand. My gaze riveted on Ed's big belt buckle. I looked up into those clear, blue eyes and then suddenly realized why Ed was walking along with the cattle— he could no longer ride. This was a shock that would have made any cowboy feel like it was the smash of the gunman's bullets. Ed Davis long ago passed his salad days, and it hurt.

As I walked along the country lane with Ed, I dared not look at him, and I couldn't speak. The cattle were a blur in my misty eyes as they hurried past. Somehow I had to hide the tears.

Ed Davis there beside me, with the bridle reins in his hand, and me with Smoke brought the whole West into sharp focus. The outdoors, the plains, the prairies, the meadows, and folks like Ed Davis represented the whole world to me and our ranching family. Ranching was a way of life that took years to seep into the core. It branded a man as surely as he branded the calf.

Ed and I were in the country lane less than half a mile from the meadow pasture. We walked slowly among the cattle who would soon turn through the gate into the field. Then together we led our horses to our neighbor's ranch headquarters.

I helped Ed unsaddle his horse and put the gear away. There was nothing to say. I shook Ed's hand, swung up on Smoke, and turned into the lane to head for home. The only sound was the click of iron horseshoes on rocks in the narrow gravel road. Smoke and I watched for the lamplight at the ranch house. Soon dusk would become another Montana night.

branding iron

It was early morning. The sky was clear and dawn was almost here. We rode down the lane to the pasture where the cattle had been driven. The cows and their calves would be taken along this lane to the ranch corrals. The branding fire had been lit, and by the time we got the cattle to the corrals it would be hot.

As we turned the cattle into the small pasture and the corrals, they became a bawling, noisy mob. The half-wild cows were now wide-eyed and belligerent. No cowboy would have wanted to be among them on foot. The gate to the branding corral was open and the cows charged through. The pole-fenced lane along the corral fence narrowed, and at its end the gate was so arranged that the calves might be turned into the small branding corral and the cows into a pasture. There were almost a hundred calves in the corral and a half-dozen branding irons in the wood fire (propane is used these days). The calves were big and strong, and a man's strength would soon be gone without the help of the wise, old cow ponies.

One cowboy looped his rope around a calf's neck; a rider looped his rope about the calf's hind legs. In a minute the calf was stretched out close to the fire. Two front legs and one hind leg were bound together, and the calf was helpless as he awaited his fate.

First there was a needle in the shoulder and he was vaccinated for anthrax, or blackleg, as the disease was known among ranchers. The acrid smoke of burned hide and hair filled the air, and a blue haze drifted about the fire. A screaming bawl left no doubt that the mark is painful.

Ed Davis whipped out his razor-sharp knife and with a few deft strokes separated the young bull from his testicles. One

Preparing for branding, Frank Perrault on far right, about 1940

more slice and a piece of hide on the left side of the animal's neck was laid open. A handful of corral dust was tossed into this cut, and the cowboys were ready for the next calf. The corral dust kept the hide from growing back; instead it would curl up into a knot. The calf now had a well-known brand and a mark denoting ownership.

The gate was opened and the stiff, bewildered calf, in great discomfort—once a bull and now a steer—hobbled through, guided by a cowboy. His hind legs were splotched with blood and his loud bawl was plaintive as he searched for his mother.

The routine was repeated again and again as the day wore on. Only the heifer calves, who did not need to be docked, changed the pace. More wood, more fire, more serum. We all traded off, save Ed. It was going to be a long day; noon had come and gone as we traded around and went to the house to eat. Now branding became a race against the dark.

The cow ponies knew exactly what to do. One rider wrapped his reins around his saddle horn and rolled a Bull Durham cigarette as the horse pulled a calf to the fire. He rose in the stirrups and struck a match on the thigh of his jeans.

Branding cows on the ranch, about 1940

The blue smoke was little different from that of the burning calfhide.

There were only a few calves and cows left in the corral; most of the others had mothered up in the holding pasture. I eased Smoke through the cattle. It would soon be nightfall, and tomorrow we would take all the cattle back to the pasture.

The yearlings and the calves who came along late in the summer and early fall were also in the main herd. Throughout the winter when the weather was good, the late summer and early fall calves were often roped in the fields, castrated, and marked, but now we had to tend to those that we missed. They had to be dehorned if their horns were more than two inches long. As the herd passed down the alleyway, those cattle were turned into another corral separate from the cows and spring calves.

Day two of branding was not like handling spring calves. The young cattle with horns were hazed along a narrow chute that had a vise made of vertical poles at the end. When the animal stuck its head out, the poles were squeezed together around his neck and he was held fast. One cowboy then had the task of putting the nose pliers on the critter and pulling his head around. Another cowboy placed the horn cutters—almost the same as bolt cutters—over one horn. Horns had to be cut off very close to the skull or they would continue to grow, possibly into deformed shapes. Badly cut horns had been known, in poorly cared-for cattle, to grow into and put out an eye.

When the horn was cut, blood squirted in a tiny stream for several feet. The hot blood hit both the holder of the critter and the dehorner. Dehorning was a disagreeable task. However, cattle with horns were dangerous to each other and heavily discounted by cattle buyers. When the horns were finally cut off, the stumps were daubed with a healthy gob of pine tar.

This seems a cruel part of cattle ranching, yet there's not much fuss on the part of the victim. On one day, however, we dehorned a two-year-old steer that had probably strayed from our range for a year. When the chute opened, he walked a few feet and fell dead. I looked at the red blood on my shirt. Sometimes ranching is hard.

In a few days we would head for the mountains and summer range. June had turned the corner and summer was on the way. As I rode along the country road toward home, my thoughts were on those mountain lands and the birds and animals that lived there.

After branding, the cattle were fed as much hay as they would eat. We wanted them well-fed because summer range was a long way from this valley, and in early spring, grass was not found everywhere along the trail. Then, too, those calves had to recover from their experiences in the branding corral.

For the trip to summer range, the horses must be shod and made ready. The young colts must be ridden every day. A cowboy must be able to stay up there or he would never find out if those colts would drive cattle and become cow horses.

The chuck wagon must be made ready for the long journey over rough and rutted country roads, most of the trip would be along the old toll road. The wagon had made the trip to summer range and back again many times. It was a pioneer wagon, a duplicate of those oaken-hooped and canvas-covered prairie schooners of Oregon Trail days. Inside there was a small sheet-iron stove with a tin pipe stuck a few inches above the canvas top. The wagon box fit between and above the wagon wheels, but extended out about one foot on each side, which made the space considerably useful. Along the inside, on the stove side, several cabinets had been installed. They

A calf is tied up for branding and castration

held the tableware and some small pots and pans, along with salt and sometimes pepper, sugar, flour, other items for cooking, and baking powder and chokecherry syrup for the biscuits and hotcakes. There were other foodstuffs and coffee, packaged for a rough ride, in safe places inside the chuck wagon. At the end of that palace of wood and canvas was a bunk. It had a mattress, which was filled with new straw every year, a patchwork, wool-filled comforter, and woolen blankets. The tent and bedrolls for night campgrounds were stored on this bunk.

The outside of the chuck wagon was a bit different from the prairie schooner. Over the tailgate of the wagon box was a makeshift stall that hung three or four feet out behind the wagon. The stall floor was covered with straw and had sides about three feet high and a removable panel at the end. This stall was the accommodation for those little calves who got too tired along the trail, and for them it was a free ride.

There was a long box along one side of the wagon that held the spuds, turnips, carrots, and other storable vegetables. Near one end, this box had been partitioned off with spaces to hold enough beans, ham, and bacon for several trips.

The horses' oat barrel, which had once been a water barrel on a prairie schooner, was lashed to the side of the wagon. In the oats were fresh eggs, which sometimes got broken. Broken eggs didn't bother horses at all: They like them raw.

There were hooks along the wagon box on both sides. When the wagon was ready to go up the trail, Dutch ovens and cast-iron skillets and the black, sooty coffee pot and other tools of the trade dangled along. The stove in the wagon would see little, if any, fire. We preferred an outside campfire and bed of coals for the Dutch ovens.

As soon as we got that chuck wagon limousine all fixed up and provisioned and its axles greased, we were ready to hook the team of horses onto the oaken tongue with the neck yoke and doubletree, and head up the trail.

Branding was the last of spring cowboy chores, and with it out of the way we would soon begin a cattle drive with real cowboys and horses. Tonight we would sleep and dream of the drive that would begin with tomorrow's early daylight—a drive just like the ones Grandfather made—which would bring those mountains far in the distance to just an arm's length away.

cattle trail

The gate was opened, and the old steer switched what was left of his tail and turned his head from side to side, quitting the bunch when he saw the open gate. Those old range-wise cows knew where that steer was heading, and they had no intention of being left behind. Smoke knew too, and his ears twitched as though on a pivot. It took a steady hand to hold him. The other cowboys stirred up the resting cattle who were not quite ready to start. As the cattle began to move out, the lowing of the cows and the bawling of the calves became intense and filled the air with western music.

The steer was now out the gate and a scattered column of cattle followed. All were casting looks about for the safety of their offspring. I headed the lead into the field at Silver Spring. We would camp along the lane ahead of the cattle the first night, but later we would camp behind them as they became strung out for miles ahead of us, feeding as they went.

It was midafternoon; the sun was bright and the sky was clear. The chuck wagon was a mile or so from the campsite. By dark all the cattle would be in the field, which would mean the end of this easy day. I kept Smoke in camp that night so that we could catch fresh horses for the trail tomorrow.

The sun was low, the evening air crisp, and the lane was a mass of lowing cows and bellering calves. The little calves who got a free ride were lifted out of the chuck wagon boot and herded toward the cattle. Cows and calves were all searching for each other.

The drag riders stripped their saddles and their gear and turned their horses loose. They walked the few yards to where the chuck wagon and the camp would be set up for the night. I took one last ride through the cattle and closed the gate.

When I returned, I left Smoke with the other horses, held by a halter rope and the drag rope. He was busy with his oats and would soon be joined by the chuck wagon team to settle in for the first trail camp.

The camp tent had been pitched and the lantern hung inside on the ridge pole. It was dark enough to see the yellow spot through the tent canvas. The other cowboys already had graniteware plates and were working on spuds, biscuits, and the remnants of big steaks. The fire was a gleaming bed of coals with Dutch oven bails sticking up. The old graniteware coffee pot rested near the edge of the fire, and the aroma of hot coffee—set against the smells of human and horse sweat—was strong.

The cook handed me a cup of coffee with one hand and with the other laid a steak over the glowing coals for a minute or two. Then he cast a bit of salt on it and flipped it over with a long-handled fork. Again he sprinkled salt, and then placed a hunk of butter in the middle. He speared a spud from the coals and dropped the steak alongside it on the graniteware plate. I reached into the Dutch oven by the fire for a biscuit. Now began the day's best work.

For a while everyone was quiet. The feast was over and the cowboys on the drag had roll-your-own Bull Durham smokes glowing. With every pull blue smoke curled skyward.

A bucket of water sat by the coals and a bar of homemade soap waited on a block to wash the dishes—that is, if you could make the soap lather. That soap would clean your hands—skin and all—unless you were awful tough.

The rope around the bedroll snapped loose with a sharp pull, and the canvas cover flipped open. Patchwork quilts over a pair of woolen blankets were now the day's best news. I smelled burning kerosene in the dim lantern light of the tent that would be our home for the night. Once the shirt, boots, and pants were off it is a second and a jump before lying between the wool blankets.

The alarm went off, and it was no metallic sound. I had not been to sleep at all, at least I didn't think so. This alarm was a long and plaintive bawl, which would soon be joined by others. The cattle were ready to go. Before we'd heard a half-dozen bawls we were wide awake and half dressed. I looked outside. Snow had put a white hat on all the fenceposts and the whole outdoors was fresh and incredibly clean. As we dressed we had to be careful not to touch the sagging, damp tent roof. It would leak wherever it was touched.

There is only time to find out how cold Silver Spring really is. This was the fastest wash ever made, but the sun will warm up today and maybe tonight the dirt will come off easier. Anyone who was not wide awake after that dip would have to have been stone dead. Unless you were careful, you might freeze while bathing.

Silver Spring was originally called Cold Spring. It was large and indeed cold, and it flowed through the beds of the Ruby Mountains into the Ruby River. It was truly a wonder of the valley. There was little water anywhere in the Ruby Mountains, but Silver Spring had as much water flowing in it as all the small streams of the Ruby Mountains put together. When the pioneer settlers began to farm the land and to raise grain, the spring was harnessed to provide power for a flour mill. The mill has been silent for many years, though the milling machinery is still inside the large building. This was one of the first flour mills in Montana, and it was important in the development of the Ruby Valley.

The snow was wet and heavy and the horses had some patches of it on their backs. I caught Smoke, curried, and brushed him. As I held the halter rope I knew that Smoke was perfectly gentle, as cow horses go. But a silver shoe turned up on the hind foot could have put a cowboy out of business in a wink. My father would not allow anyone to saddle and ride a horse that was not properly cared for, and I was no exception. By the time Smoke had eaten his oats I would be ready to saddle up.

The saddle and blanket were under the wagon. The blanket fit fine, but the saddle was some two or three inches off Smoke's back in the rear and didn't fit this cool morning. Snow seems to curve the sway in horses backs the wrong way. I was able to cinch up the saddle, but just barely. No sense in making a bad situation worse. Snow is soft to land on but the snow today is almost as wet as water, and I've already washed once. I decided to just walk a way and get my feet warm, and then maybe the saddle would fit a little better.

When I climbed up, and after Smoke turned around a couple of times, the rock under the saddle seemed to melt away. The old steer and some of the old cows were waiting at the gate, ready to go. When the gate was opened those nearest rushed out, and soon the whole field was moving about and coming toward the gate. By the time I caught the loose horses, those cattle would be headed up the trail. Now that the lead had gone up the lane, there would soon be a race to see who got to summer range first, but by tomorrow the trail would all slow down.

I dropped a rope on a fresh horse for the drag rider and then made a halter and tied the horse to the fence. Then I followed the cattle along to the chuck wagon and led the fresh horses. The cattle thinned out past the chuck wagon. They knew the way and they seldom looked back or turned their eyes away from the distant mountains.

The smoke of the campfire made a thin plume of blue over the chuck wagon. The coffee pot was in the fire. By the time I got off Smoke there was a cup of coffee sitting on a block near the fire for me. There was bacon in one long-handled skillet, and in another a buttermilk pancake. The drag riders had eaten and were busy saddling up. They would work along the cattle, check the field to be sure we had them all, and coax along a few little calves.

The calves had faces so white they looked like they had just been scrubbed. Their noses looked like bitterroot flowers. Some of the littlest ones would soon need a ride in the boot of the chuck wagon. The calves looked fragile and shaky, but we all knew they were as strong as Nature could make them.

Finished with breakfast, I picked my way among the cattle to the lead, past the chuck wagon, which was lurching along the rutted road. The cows and the older calves picked a bite of new grass anywhere they could as they moseyed along. The old steer and the cows in the lead were nowhere in sight. It would be an hour before I caught them and made sure they were on the right road. Most likely I would have to hold them back a bit so that the herd would not be scattered too far by nightfall. They were beginning to quiet down, and by camp tonight the drag at the end of the cattle herd would be eight or ten miles from the first camp, Silver Spring.

The next day the trail and the cattle drive would pass through the village of Laurin, Montana. Laurin was first called Cicero, but the name was later changed in honor of Jean Baptiste Laurin, one of Montana's earliest merchants.

Laurin came to Cicero on July 15, 1863, two months after the discovery of gold in Alder Gulch. He had been an Indian trader for years, and he opened a store in a canvas house. The store and some other enterprises were immensely successful. He soon became a wealthy landowner and a toll bridge operator. Cicero—which had once been bounty land given to a soldier—then became the village of Laurin.

Laurin lay in the heart of the Ruby Valley, which was then one of the last wild and unclaimed regions in the nation. The Bannock Indians came to this valley for centuries before the lands were ceded by Chief Tendoy to the "Great White Father" in Washington, D.C. In J. B. Laurin's store, Tendoy signed the treaty permanently transferring the lands. After this, the Bannocks left their land in the Ruby Valley for the Lemhi Indian reservation in Idaho, and the plow, the harrow, and barbed wire came to take their place.

I was on Smoke as the trail herd crossed the historic Stinkingwater River bridge into the village of Laurin, directly in front of J. B. Laurin's pioneer store and a famous cottonwood tree.

It was on this bridge that the Montana vigilantes held a trial for suspected road agents Brown and Yeager on January 4, 1864. On that winter's day the road agents were convicted and hanged in a cold wind from the cottonwood tree until dead. The tree still stands.

The new and beautiful hand-hewn stone Catholic church, made from limestone quarried nearby, replaced the original Catholic church where my grandparents were married. It was a gift to the town from J. B. Laurin upon his death.

The old steer moseyed up the country road through all that history, leading the herd behind him. Buildings in Laurin circled a sort of plaza. The frontier store faced east, with meadow sod in front of it. Across the plaza and east of the church were the Northern Pacific Railroad tracks.

Those tracks brought back a memory fragment from a boyhood event—a train ride from Sheridan to Laurin. Grandmother held my hand as the huge black monster breathing steam went past the platform. Finally the handsome passenger coach stopped a few feet from the station platform. The door opened, and the conductor set a small stool before the stair leading to the coach so we could climb aboard.

Inside, a beautiful curved and decorated ceiling flowed down into large windows. A potbellied, Round Oak stove at the end of the coach had a coal-filled hod with a shiny brass spittoon nearby. There was no fire, for it was summer. The seats were bright red velvet, softer than a barebacked horse. They had fancy curved armrests made of iron and trimmed in gold. There were fancy footrests, too.

Grandmother wore a lace-trimmed hat with tiny flowers. Her wide blue eyes and a wisp of still-dark hair set her face off perfectly. Grandmother's hat had a pin with a sparkling stone as big as a magpie egg on one end.

With a sharp jerk, a bunch of clatter, a lot of chugging, a huge burst of steam, a bell ringing, and a deafening blast of the steam whistle, the train began to move. I thought the noise and clatter meant the whole train was falling apart; and I felt like I was inside on a monster without a saddle. I grabbed the fancy armrests and hung on for dear life.

Once the door closed, the clatter dimmed and the click of iron wheels on wavy track told me we were under way. A huge cloud of steam passed the window. The coach shook and brakes squealed, and the melodious voice of the conductor sang out, "Looray."

Looking around as I came out of my daydream, I saw that most of the trail herd had passed Laurin, and it would mean some hurry to catch up with the lead again and head for the coming night's camp at the Caswell place. We had to pass Alder—a few miles beyond Laurin and the last of the towns and villages on the drive—in a hurry. Alder is the last town on the rickety railroad, too. It is a jumble of dilapidated buildings and houses on both sides of the road and was the home of the Buffalo Hump Saloon.

Alder was always a hard place to get those half-wild cattle through without a show. One of the steady customers at the Buffalo Hump Saloon always chose the wrong time to cross the narrow street. Last year a customer came out, stopped in the middle of the road, and doffed his hat with a great flourish just as the half-wild cows came close. Well, gathering fifty or so cattle from among the buildings and chasing that fellow back into the Buffalo Hump took most of the afternoon. The spectacle of those saloon patrons laughing and yelling their encouragement at the yearly show in Alder was not our idea of a good time.

Today would be a different show in Alder. We were all close behind the lead and the cows were obviously watching to see what the old steer would do. They seemed to remember what went on here last year.

The swinging doors of the Buffalo Hump opened and our special helper leisurely proceeded to the middle of the street, directly before the cattle. The old steer and the cows stopped and stood still for a couple of seconds. When the fellow doffed his hat to bow, we went to work. The audience wasn't ready for our yells and commotion, and departed in a matter of seconds—or at least got out of sight. The hat was no longer sitting on the fellow's head, but was on the ground in the middle of the street. The fellow himself was making tracks for the Buffalo Hump with the old steer right behind him, gaining fast. In another few seconds the old steer and some of the cows were inside the saloon and ready for a shot of white lightning, along with their hatless friend.

We sat on our horses, watching and waiting to see what would happen. The front doors had disappeared and the racket inside sounded almost like someone chopping wood. In only a minute or two, we saw daylight through the back door. Later we found out that there was now a lot of vacant space in that saloon for dancing. We gathered up the old steer and wild cows and proceeded on up the road to summer range. The hat in the street had new dents in it, and was now painted green.

We had little to do for a while except just ride along the string of cattle and be part of the country we lived in. Some would have said that the cattle drive was hard work, but I doubt anyone here would have agreed. Cowboys clamored for a chance to soak up some trail dust. There was open range past the wild meadows along the Ruby River. The Ruby Valley would pinch out a few miles ahead to the south of where the river flowed through a notch in the canyon—the site of the old toll gate on Pete Daley's toll road. At the edge of the canyon we would make our last camp in the valley.

There was new grass starting everywhere along the lane, but only a few spring blooms on the plants. The birch on the riverbank had tiny green leaves. The cottonwoods were a delicate yellow-green. Their great trunks were white with black-squared lines on them. When we returned there would be cotton in the air and the sap would ooze out of every tiny pore along the limbs. The odor of spring perfume would be everywhere.

A wedge of ducks was too nervous to paddle around the pond so close to the cattle. We could see a pair of mallards not quite hidden by the cattails. They either had a nest nearby, or likely already had a nervous eye upon a flock of little ducklings.

A pair of swamp hawks swirled almost effortlessly near the cattle, in hopes that mice or rabbits would be scared from their hiding places and become the birds' dinner. When they did see a rodent, they dropped like a bullet and were only on the ground a second or two before flying away with some hapless victim.

Most interesting of all was a coyote standing among the cattails. Since we were quiet and careful to not move, and the cattle and horses are just other outdoor beasts to him, he paid us no mind as he stood at attention with one foot raised. A quick dart and the coyote tossed a field mouse almost six feet into the air and then deftly caught it as it fell. Now he had his dinner— or at least dessert.

There were meadowlarks on almost every fencepost, singing their spring songs. There were a few flocks of blackbirds; some, the larger ones, with red patches on their wings. Many of the blackbirds seemed tied to the cattail stalks and willows along the ponds and swamps by the river. Tomorrow we would leave the lower valley and begin the climb into the mountains and summer range.

The day wore on and the chuck wagon was nearing the evening camp. Several cows were following closely behind to be sure none of the little calves in the boot would get lost. Now and then we needed to push some slowpoke, and once in a while we needed to point some yearling on the way to summer range. The tension of the past two days was gone: All the cattle had adjusted to the trail and were content to feed as they went along.

The Caswell house was made of round cobblestones. That might be nice for summer, but we always speculated about what Montana blizzard winter days were like in a stone house. Just past the house, the Ruby River flowed through the canyon notch, and then the fences disappeared. Somewhere along the river were some lost graves, one of which held the remains of trapper Vanderburg of the American Fur Company, a fierce competitor of Jim Bridger. Vanderburg was among the first to trap beaver on the Ruby. He was killed by Indians along with one of his men.

From the hill south of our camp, the high peaks of the Snowcrests and Gravelly Range outlined summer range ahead. The river held the cattle on the west, but the east was open range. Tomorrow we would do a lot more riding to gather the drag and to be sure none of the cattle had wandered into side canyons. We would keep an eye out for sleeping calves behind sagebrush back along the trail.

It was near dusk when we made our final approach to the campsite, behind the cattle. It was slower now because some of the cattle were getting tired and we had to help keep the families together. The cows would be looking for their calves, and they wanted to go back to where the calves last nursed. That is Nature's way of keeping them together. Even though the snow was but one day gone, the road was dusty and there was a lot of confusion in the drag. Heifers were tired; some, perhaps tonight, would have little calves. They were slow and would like to be away from the herd. There were a lot of tired calves, too.

The cowboys had a rope on a most unhappy cow, but the cook needed some milk, and it would not be a great loss to her. I was busy catching the loose horses among the cattle. We had fashioned a rope corral for the horses and they were busy with their oats. Someone would ride through the drag and on up the road a piece to be sure all is well, then this day's work would be done.

We would all ride fresh horses tomorrow. The three colts were not cow horses yet, (one trail does not make a cow horse) but they would be when we got home in a few days.

The colts were taking a good look at the rope corral and a side-long glance at the hay, but any notions they had would change with oats. Tomorrow these colts would join the other cow ponies who considered this trail old hat. As the mountains came ever closer, we began to see sage, pine, fir trees, and juniper. A pungent odor filled the springtime air along the trail, and we were in a new world in Montana.

from the valley to the mountains

The country along the trail drive was open, with no springs or mountain creeks. The river was close by, and we rode there to wash up and water the horses. The chuck wagon was parked on an open slope with no trees nearby, only sagebrush. The coffee pot was steaming, and the odor of hot coffee mingled with that of burning sage, cow chips, and wood.

The river was just as cold as Silver Spring had been, but there was no snow. Just to show how tough we really were we all did the necessary, but not too carefully, and right quick. One could bet his wage, if he had one, that the coffee would taste a lot better after that. There were two Dutch ovens in the fire that night and the old granite plates were leaned against a log near the fire. The cook relieved the Dutch ovens of their lids, and biscuits, beans, and ham filled the air with odors found only in heaven. Food cooked like this, on the trail camp-fire, has a story of its own.

The story of the ham began the winter before. My uncle put bacon and the hams in oak barrels to cure in a brine that was the valley's most perfect recipe, or so he testified. The half-century-old oak barrels came from Kansas. After the hams and bacon were taken from the brine, they were hung in the smokehouse. My job was to keep a smoky fire of applewood and birch going all the time. When the time was right, the hams and bacon were hung in the original homestead cabin. With its log walls and dirt roof, it was the perfect cooler. When the hams and bacon were ready for the table, we got to taste the secret recipe. It was some of that ham that we were eating tonight.

After dinner we turned in early again, using our pants and shirts for pillows. When dawn broke, the mournful lowing of the cattle was right next to camp. The horses waited in the rope corral for their oats. Today I would ride the bay colt who had an interesting history. A classmate of the wartime president Woodrow Wilson came to this great open country with several Thoroughbred race horses. He met an untimely death and the horses were turned loose on the open range of the prairie. That bay horse, with his Thoroughbred lines, Roman nose, white star on his forehead, and one front leg white almost to the knee, was no doubt related to those Thoroughbreds, most likely the offspring of a range mare and a Thoroughbred stud. Any horse more than two years old and unbranded belonged to the man who could brand him, and we had caught and branded him, so he was ours.

One thing about the bay horse—when you get up on him you'd better have some place to go or else you were going to be left behind. Before we could eat breakfast, we had to go most of ten miles to reach the old steer and the cows in the lead. Riding through the cattle before they got moving made it much easier to see that all was well. By now we knew all the cattle, but another rider would also go through them to double-check that they were all there and all right.

Nature provides range cattle with the ability to cope with almost any condition, in many ways they exhibited the traits of wild animals. The folks who lived outdoors among the animals soon learned to read those traits.

After we returned and had breakfast, I helped the cook hook up his team. The chuck wagon would wind its way up the country road and set up at Ice Creek, closer to the timbered mountains, by late afternoon. I rode along through the cattle, with a yell or two at those not moving, and edged them along the way. There were about fifty head that had turned up a small canyon for some new grass. It took most of an hour to get them back to the trail. One small calf had crawled into the thick brush to hide. The bay colt was busy watching the calf, and when the calf saw he was being watched, he rushed out of the brush—his tail high in the air, at a dead run—and headed for the cattle and his mother. The cattle were stringing out past the buffalo jumps, about eight miles past last night's camp. We were traveling over artifacts left from the buffalo that the Indians drove over the cliffs. In another mile we would pass the old toll road that crosses the river and then continues on the old pioneer road.

By the time we reached camp, the old cows and old steer in the lead would be headed for the Three Forks of the Ruby River, where three small streams came together from the basins of the high mountains of summer pasture. The headquarters, corrals, and cabin for the Ruby-range rider were at the forks. Early in the afternoon we would head the cattle off and hold them at the forks to rest for a few days, then we would go up the trail and over the divide into the Centennial Valley. In the open range close to the camp, the cattle spread out and fed along the roadsides as they slowly moved.

The cattle were now taking the trail like it was an everyday occurrence, they were much quieter and content to take a bit of grass here and there. The mothers of the little calves carried in the chuck wagon boot were scattered throughout the trail herd. I'd have to bring them back closer to their offspring. Once the cows and calves got together we could forget them for the day. Nature's bond between cow and calf was much stronger than man's interference, and we only needed to see that the bond had a chance to work.

Ice Creek was only about a foot wide and named wrong for sure. It was only springtime, but the water was already as warm as tea. The sun was still an hour from setting and there was no fence to be seen here.

The colts were getting tired from the cow-horse training lessons. There were some twenty or thirty cattle between Gus and me when suddenly Gus's colt exploded without warning. On the first jump Gus flew as high as the stirrups let him go— you could see daylight over the backs of the cows between Gus and me. When he came down he was in front of the saddle. The next jump and he came down behind the saddle and then flew off the right side of the wildly-bucking and scared colt. Cattle scattered everywhere, and when things finally cleared Gus was hanging alongside the horse with his foot fast in the stirrup. If the colt went to kicking, Gus might have been seriously hurt or killed.

There was no way to get hold of the furiously-bucking horse from the back of the colt I was riding, who was far from gentle. I jumped off my horse and headed over to Gus and the bucking colt, but the problem of getting Gus free from the stirrup still remained. Fortunately, when I was almost in reach of the pair, Gus fell free. Thankfully, he was okay. We led the colt while Gus limped along. Then Gus got back up there, so the colt wouldn't get the notion that he could dump anyone off whenever he felt like it.

We limped into camp and put the two colts in the rope corral with the other horses, who were already eating their oats. The rope corral consisted of one rope tied from wagon, to post, to tree, and so on. It was meant to hold those trail horses who had been along the road several times and to whom the hay and oats were worth more than the grass outside.

All of the drag was past us and there was some lowing and bawling from the cows and calves that were still separated. The old bulls surveyed this scene with no sound and no apparent concern, and indifferently nibbled on the grass within easy reach. By dark that night the cattle would be quiet and most would be mothered up, except for a possible heifer or two that was not used to the trail or motherhood.

We built a real fire and sat about on logs left at this campsite in years past. Smoke from the fire's still-damp wood rose lazily into the sapphire sky. There was little talk—we were content to rest, contemplate the day's events, and wait for the Dutch ovens to get hot. Tomorrow would be fir, juniper, sage, and a new outdoors.

The flames were gone now, and the sun was just a glow above the horizon. The granite plates were warm and the lids came off the Dutch ovens. We each got a couple of sourdough biscuits covered with cowboy stew—spuds, turnips, rutabagas, carrots, onions, chunks of beef, and gravy—that would please a king. It made no difference how hungry one could get, you simply couldn't hold enough out on that trail.

I recalled the story of how, there at Ice Creek camp many years ago, when Father was about six years old and on his first trail ride, he'd had a nightmare and had run off into the sagebrush with some of the cowboys in fast pursuit. Now the lantern was glowing in the open tent and the odor of burned kerosene filled the air. It was a sure sign that the day was done and sleep would come as fast as deer—or my father—could run.

three forks cow camp

The first cow bawled, and then another, and another, even though it was still fairly dark, with only a shaft or two of light in the east above the mountaintop. I heard a coyote yip and then an answer, followed by a whole orchestra of coyotes.

We were in the foothills before a high mountain at Ice Creek, and we would start a gentle climb today. We would still be able to see the river, not losing it until we finally passed Three Forks. The meadows along the river were small and narrow, the cottonwood trees few and not very large. Willows all along the river were just getting green and the birch of the valley would soon be lost to the mountain red willows and the green-barked willows of the river. Delicate green quaking aspen could be seen in the little draws; mountain sinkholes were mixed with some snowbanks here and there. Now that the aspen were beginning to leaf out, there was a feeling of spring in the mountain air.

From camp at Ice Creek the road traversed the east mountain slope. We would round this bench and then drop into a mountain basin along the river. We rode those colts again, for if we didn't we could have a rodeo in one of those mountain places, with an audience of mountain animals and half-wild Hereford cows.

When breakfast was over and the cook's team and chuck wagon were ready, we saddled up the frisky colts. Maybe this mountain air agreed too well with them, but they would come in tired at dusk. I mounted carefully, with the left rein tight enough to pull the bay's head around, and had a smooth and easy lift to the saddle seat. A spur across the hip would sure have caused a colt to come unglued. After he had turned around a couple of times and couldn't get his head down, we headed for the cattle in the lead.

Cattle on the summer range

As we rode I got those cattle that were lying down and those that were feeding to move. The calves took the notion to bawl and look for some warm milk. The trail-wise cows soon moved out, and a mile from camp they moseyed over the hillside, grazing as they went along the sides of the old pioneer road. The cattle soon strung out for at least five or six miles in small groups and in pairs of cows and calves, and the whole road seemed to move.

At noon the old steer and the cows in the lead came into view. They were almost ready to drop down into the basin at the forks. There was feed in this basin, some left from last fall and some new spring growth. We would hold all the cattle here for a few days to rest up, and let them feed and get their bellies full. Then would come the push through the larkspur on the south rim, past Poison Creek, and on to summer range.

It was a beautiful spring day with the air clear and sharp. The sun was warm and the shadows of the trees were etched on the ground so that the outline of each limb could be clearly seen.

My horse seemed to sense something I couldn't hear or see. His ears turned first this way and then that, then toward me as though I might be the cause. I pulled the colt up and sat dead still in the saddle, and then I heard the notes of "Little Joe the Wrangler" float over the hill. This was spring trail, and another rider was happy, too.

As the cattle spilled out across the mountain basin there was time to marvel at this place. The brush along the river-banks was thick and contorted and the cottonwood trees, some leaning far out over the river, were just beginning to leaf out. Brush and tree limbs were broken from the loads of winter snow. The meadows along the river had lots of grass, and some of last year's crop was still standing. Sage and buffalo grass could be seen on the higher slopes. The sharp aroma of spring was everywhere, mingled with the smell of fir and pine and a few junipers. In places there were groves of lodgepole pine and here and there a ponderosa pine towering over the sage. The mountaintops were white with snow, but the craggi-est cliffs were bare. On the south rim, just a bit higher than the meadows there at Three Forks, was larkspur.

We were in the land of mountain beasts and birds. Swamp hawks, magpies, eagles, killdeer, and a few meadowlarks were prominent, as in the lower valleys. Crows here were big black ravens, and the owls were the big hooting kind. Mountain bluebirds joined the robins and the wrens flying from tree to tree. Close by, in the clumps of juniper and sage, was a host of sage grouse. Raucous camp robbers and mountain blue jays screamed as we rode by.

There were lots of mice in the mountain meadows and about the slopes of the rolling hills, and they were the main diet of the many coyotes. Gopher towns, along with scattered badger holes, dotted the hillsides. There were no rattlesnakes here, though often along the creeks and in the river meadows a bright, striped water snake would hurry out of your path.

Many coyotes were about, but the country was so open, and the sage so thick, they were often not seen. It seemed as though all the coyotes sang together in the mornings and in the evenings, especially in the cool spring and fall weather. In the old days wolves also made this land their home; but it is a fair guess that it was one of the last wolves here that got a piece of that old steer's tail, and that happened more than ten years ago.

On the rim past the forks, we would likely see both deer and elk along the trail. Mule deer liked the tall sage, and one needed a sharp eye to see the does and their fawns at this time of year. The meadow in the mountains was just a step between the valley below and the next higher level. The old pioneer road connected farther south with the Oregon Trail across the Continental Divide. It was beginning to green up, but it would be another month before the high mountain meadows of summer would be in full bloom.

The chuck wagon had been pulled across the road below the forks to keep the cattle from heading back toward the valley. The cattle would scatter out along the meadows near the river and on the lower slopes where the grass was. In the early spring the short, new grass had less food value than later in the summer. Nevertheless, the cattle would rest up, eat their fill, and be content.

The range rider's cabin at Three Forks had been witness to many cattle drives and roundups, with a few rodeos thrown in. Three Forks of the Ruby River had been the headquarters for the upper Ruby Range for many years. Even then, half a century or more since the first use of those great grasslands in the Gravelly Mountains, they were still premium livestock ranges. Ranchers still grazed their cattle in common herds of several thousand on lands that saw almost no fences, except at the headquarters. Once they were on those great open ranges, the cattle would mix. They would spend the summer in grass that scraped their bellies, resting along some creek or by some spring, chewing their cuds, and becoming fat.

In the fall, the ranchers would gather the cattle at the forks and split them into individual ownerships, a process that took almost a month. Then the individual herds would again be on their way home to the valley and the owners' ranches.

What stories the logs of this forks cabin could tell! How many boots had marked the pine floor—how many cowboys had spent time there with the aches, pains, and sprains they'd gotten from some half-broke cow horse? How many rains, how many snows, and, of course, how many of those famous Montana blizzards has this cabin weathered? As time went on, the many experiences the cowboys had here would become embossed with fancy dreams rather than actual facts.

Frank Perrault surrounded by white-faced Herefords on the Perrault Ranch, with Old Baldy Mountain in the background

Memories are short, and bad and painful experiences soon cover over with a blanket of happiness on a spring day in the sunshine. It was good to be alive, and to be sitting on a good horse with all of Nature's gifts at hand.

The cast-iron stovetop was hot, real hot, blue hot. The oven door was open and there were lots of freshly baked spuds inside. A handful of salt was cast across the hot stovetop and the sizzle of thick beef steaks could be heard for a minute or two. The cook flipped them over and put a hunk of butter in the middle. When the butter melted, the steaks were done. We were now so hungry we could hardly wait to hold the old graniteware plates with the steaks, the baked spuds, and a cup of hot coffee. We went to work with a knife and fork as soon as we sat around on the old straw-mattress beds. We could watch the road through the open cabin door until the evening meal was finished.

A mule deer doe and a tiny fawn tiptoed ever so carefully into the meadow, forsaking the safety of the river brush. The doe took a few steps and then cautiously surveyed the landscape, her great ears turning every which way. Her fawn was never very far from her. The nighthawks of the prairie did not like the high country, and I missed the evening sails of those birds as we watched the deer.

It was now almost dark and the cabin had been lighted, after a fashion, by the lantern. The old beds made good places to sit and listen to the tales of other days at Three Forks cow camp as coffee cups were filled to overflowing. These were stories of the rides and the rodeos, some on purpose and some quite accidental. Some years Montana weather dealt herself a hand, and those were the years folks at the camp never forgot. Frostbite left long memories. Soon it was time to turn in.

Sure as the day breaks, the old cows let us know. That morning the bawls were not urgent—there was no rush to get ready to go on up the trail. Washed up, breakfast over, the horses fed and all cared for, we saddled up. Smoke was anxious to go, as always. The old steer was up the road with some of the old trail-wise cows. We took a hike up there and spooked them back closer to the main herd. It would be a great day today in the spring sunshine. We would ride up the little canyons and draws, where a few cattle here and there would need to be brought closer to the herd. There was peace and tranquillity here that could be found nowhere else. This was the real outdoors, Montana's outdoors.

When day was almost gone, we left the rim and headed for camp. Cattle had been loosely gathered from the benches and the edge of the rim, and could be seen scattered over the meadows and along the streams. Some were resting and some were grazing or shining up their calves.

Larkspur is one of the first plants to break the soil in spring. It's bright green with leaves disguising a dreadful potion. Larkspur invites a cow to feast long before other plants have recovered from winter. This early in the new season larkspur would be short and not nearly as dangerous as later, when the vivid, beautiful purple blooms graced the stems.

We knew the larkspur patches up on the rim very well. With the cattle rested and their bellies full we would rush them past those spots. This was one place the cattle must not stop to graze or rest.

I was sitting on the log in front of the range rider's cabin, and dusk was fast returning. I waited and watched for the deer and her fawn. Sure enough, they appeared only a few feet from where they were last evening. They would spend the whole summer here, probably within a few acres of this patch of meadow.

The next day I saddled up the bay colt and headed along the west bend, forded the west fork of the river, and again checked the pass. I saw some of the yearlings along the small canyons and in the sinks, they would need to be turned back toward the main herd. Most of the little canyon slices along the slopes held tiny streams with aspen at their heads. Many still had snowbanks that would feed the streams for most of the summer.

On the pass, which was a few hundred feet above Three Forks basin, there was lots of sage and a few scattered clumps of fir and pine. Squirrels had nests in the trees and they scampered from limb to limb and scolded when I rode close. Blue jays and camp robbers scolded more fiercely and followed from tree to tree to let me know I was unwanted.

To the south, the land was a roller coaster of small, sage-covered hills and gentle valleys. Sage grouse were thick there, and sometimes more than a hundred thundered away suddenly. Occasionally, those near their nests scurried off along the ground among the sage.

To the west, blue mountains turned to a cap of white snow above timberline. Those were the Snowcrests. Snow is gone from them only a few days in late summer. East and north, the rolling hills hid more mountains.

The few small snowbanks in the trees were still on the pass but would pose no problem for cattle. We had timed the trail almost exactly. One more day and we would be over the pass and through the larkspur. In one more day, mountain range and summer for the cattle would begin. At the forks, the cattle had been pushed close together. The cows and calves were bawling—they seemed to sense that tomorrow would be the day.

cows, poison, and summer range

After breakfast the cows began to bawl and the calves to answer. We harnessed the team and hooked them to the chuck wagon. We were ready to go, too.

Smoke was standing quietly with the reins loose on the ground. The other riders were stirring up the cattle and pushing in the edges of the herd. The spare horses were in the corral; we'd need them in a couple of hours or so. I hoped to get a biscuit from the cook when I changed horses. As I mounted Smoke, the old lead steer and some of the cows went by at a trot. We were on our way through the larkspur and over the pass.

Swinging my rope and yelling as all cowboys do, I pushed the first fifty cattle or so into the lead and headed on up the trail. Soon we saw Poison Creek. There were Poison Creeks everywhere in the West, but this one was unusual because it was named for the larkspur, not for rattlesnakes, as most others were.

Yelling cowboys and bawling cows and calves told me that we were on our way. The cattle were bunched together more than ever before on the trail; the whole herd was not more than a few hundred yards long and less than half that distance wide.

On the pass, the landscape flattened out and the cattle scattered among the trees and giant sagebrush clumps unless we held the herd together. If they were allowed to stop and graze, some would try the larkspur, and that might be fatal. It was a day when the old steer was better than any cowboy. He just moved along, winding his way through the sagebrush and the clumps of larkspur.

The trail-wise cows were closely following the old steer and the lead cattle, and I was hurrying from one to the other so they wouldn't stop. I knew that anyone who was not familiar with the range and the trail would think a bunch of madmen were after these cattle. It was a frantic time up on the pass, with ropes snapping and a whole variety of yells. We raced from one place to another, ever watchful for the critter that would stop. There was no need for a mackinaw, even though it was cool in early morning. The sweat had turned Smoke's flanks and withers wet, and white froth outlined his breast collar. One of the other cowboys came to spell me, and I used the short time to go back to camp and get that biscuit.

The bay horse was raring to go and I did not hold him back. I helped push the drag up tight so I could head for the lead, pushing the cattle along the closely packed herd as I went. Once more at the lead and again back and forth, with ropes swinging and yells in the air, we pushed the cattle on up the trail. By early afternoon the drag cleared the rim and most of the pass, with the chuck wagon close behind the moving herd. The cook had stopped to put a couple of little calves in the chuck wagon. Today puts us at our last open country camp and close to the end of the drive.

There was a yearling steer up ahead with his head down and his back humped. He now knew the taste of larkspur and had a green apple bellyache like the one I had. Lying down and calling it quits was the easy way for him, but we kept him on the move. We would most likely find another one or two, but so far we had not lost a single critter.

Most of the cattle were past the larkspur—only a single plant here and there could be seen. We would soon cross the divide into Centennial Valley, a great, flat basin of shallow lakes, swamps, ponds, and streams. The valley was home to water, grass, swamp weeds, and cattails, among which great flocks of water birds consorted. Camp tonight would be on the pass to the north, in the sagebrush with sage grouse and coyotes.

Before the divide and off to the right sat a tiny log cabin along the old pioneer road. It was a lonely site, without trees and even without much sagebrush. The roof was dirt, with wild plants sticking up here and there. The front door faced the road. A window on each side was one log high and about a foot wide. A kind of barbed-wire fence holding a few curious goats surrounded the cabin. A thin cloud of smoke from the chimney proved that someone lived there. As we neared the cabin, a dog began to bark. That cabin home was in the middle of nowhere, cut off from the outside world for at least six months of each year by winter snows and spring mud.

The old man who came out of the cabin door was gray and bent. He wore bib overalls and a bright plaid shirt. A woman in a long gray dress stood in the door behind him, the only color a red ribbon in her hair. We knew that these folks had been in this nowhere land for many years, and the tiny cabin was their home. A small garden and the goats were the only things between them and starvation. Of course, wild game added to the larder. One could not help but wonder when the day would come that only one of these old folks would come to the door to greet us.

What had drawn them to this remote spot in the first place? Were they true pioneers who felt that a neighbor within miles was too close? Land here was once free, and there were many folks who were stuck in the vacant spaces in the open country of Montana. We always speculated about these people. These two old folks in that land of solitude were dependent upon gold panned from the small streams in the mountains. Their wealth was the luck of the placer gravels.

The chuck wagon parked a few miles farther on the trail. The creek nearby was small, and there was a flat space just off the trail in the sage-covered hills that had been the campsite for years, even before us or any pioneers. It was originally used by Indians and later by the earliest explorers, trappers, and prospectors. From that campsite it was a clear shot on to the Oregon Trail and into the Idaho country along the old pioneer road that joined the toll road across the pass.

That night's campsite was on an alkali flat with a small brook running through it. The water was not sweet or clear like most mountain streams, but small rainbow trout about six inches long were abundant and flashed about. The brook seemed to barely flow along among swamp grasses and small patches of cattails.

West and south lay the Centennial basin, filled with water-logged meadows. On the south side of the basin rose high hills that held the whole valley captive. The edge of the basin on the west and again on the east was rimmed with lakes. The sky was filled with ducks, geese, and some pairs of trumpeter swans. The water birds flew back and forth over the basin all day and night, and their cries continually filled the air.

We were almost as high there as the meadows on the summer range. As we went on south we would first drop down near the valley's edge and then climb north up the slope to summer range.

The campfire was betrayed by a plume of pine and sage smoke. The coffee pot was near the fire and we had time for some different-tasting coffee—made with alkali water—before we needed to care for the horses. Only the horses we rode over from Three Forks would be needed to finish the spring trail. From that campsite on to summer range the trail was a snap. The old steer and trail-wise cows would lead the herd almost by themselves. We could pick up the rest of the horses at the forks when we went back home.

The tent was pitched and we threw in the bedrolls. It was dusk and time to wash up and get ready for the evening meal. The food was mighty welcome because the biscuits had been used up a long time ago. Beans and ham seemed most appropriate at that old mountain campsite. I walked around camp, looking for an Indian arrowhead, without any luck. We washed the dishes and stacked them alongside the grub box. We had never heard of drying dishes on any cattle trail. I just thought a few streaks were naturally part of trail dishes—and the alkali in that creek guaranteed streaks at this camp.

We sat against the tarp hung over the wagon wheels to watch the day end, dusk turn into twilight, and the night sky fill with bright stars. It would be only a short while until the dippers graced the sky. The moon was almost full that night, and it was just now climbing over the eastern ridges. The moon and stars gave enough light so that large print could be read here. In the sack in the evening with the lantern out, the moon made a yellow spot on the tent roof. For a few minutes before sleep came, the cries of the ducks and geese and the mellow tones of the trumpeter swans could be heard. A coyote yipped on a hill close to camp and then was answered.

In the morning outside the tent, the cries of the water birds still filled the air. The breeze was clear and sharp and there was frost on the ground. The brook was nearly frozen over in the potholes.

When breakfast was over, the ride for cattle in the lead began. I could see that they were nearly to the edge of summer range, stringing out along the road. By early afternoon we would turn the cattle over to the summer range rider and begin the trip home. The pace was slow since there was no hurry. The cattle stopped frequently to graze on the short grass along the gentle slope by the road. We did not bother to disturb those that were lying down. They would get up and join the herd on their own time today.

A two-story house stood next to the country road; to the east was a meadow and a swamp full of cattails. There was an open shed that was closed on the north and covered with brush, straw, or swamp grass. In the yard was a hay mower, a rake, and a wagon, but no sign of cattle or horses, although some had to be near.

A huge fellow came toward the gate. His beard was full and touched with gray. He wore waist-length Levi's and heavy woolen underwear with long sleeves instead of a shirt. His hair was shoulder length. He was a bear of a man, over six feet tall, with great long arms and a barrel chest. He walked slowly to the gate, leaned against the post, and waved a long arm in friendly greeting. We were the first people he had seen since last fall. We shared news of the valley and watched for the six kids he supposedly had. No woman or children came to the house door or were seen anywhere. Finally, one small face appeared in the corner of a window and another in the old shed. The rest were nowhere to be seen, but they had to be somewhere. The children were shy and afraid. Perhaps our range rider would see them now and then. I wondered what would happen to those kids as they grew up in that lonesome valley.

Centennial Valley was home to only a few ranchers who cut marsh hay and ranged their cattle nearby. It was still one of the most inaccessible mountain basins in the West. Here we were truly in the great outdoors with flocks of water birds, grouse, deer, elk, and coyotes. Now we had come here to spoil that mountain paradise with our white-faced Hereford cattle.

The cattle were slowing down and spreading out along the hillside. The range rider's cabin, which would be his home that summer, was a log cabin that was once the home of another homesteader—log walls, dirt roof, and pine-board floor, knotholes and all. Situated on a gentle slope beneath the hill, the cabin afforded a view for many miles to the south and west. A stone cairn protected a spring near a dirt-and-sage-covered bank. The spring water was always in the shade and was so cold it could almost do the same job as Mom's old icebox.

We turned the horses loose in a small fenced pasture. The cabin would be stocked with food from the chuck wagon. The range rider would go back to the forks with us for the horses he needed for summer. Range season would find him spreading the cattle around the high mountain slopes and the meadow, much the same as we did on the prairie in the springtime. These slopes were the grasslands of Gravelly Range.

back to the ranch

Centennial Valley lies directly north of the Continental Divide with Monida Pass at the westerly end of the valley. It is plate flat and has been filled with the fine sediments of the hills surrounding it. The Gravelly Range lies north of the valley with rolling grasslands and scattered groves of pines and aspen— these lands are the summer range for the cattle we have trailed.

Centennial Valley is locked in snow, storms, or mud for most of the year except during the hot and dry summer months. In spring, range cattle are anxious to come to the high country. In fall, when the days begin to shorten and the nights to cool, they are ready to return to lower elevations. The half-wild range cattle are not a great deal different from the migratory buffalo.

Ranching in Centennial Valley means grazing cattle on the hillsides in the summer months and hauling swamp hay all winter long. The few permanent residents of the valley have lots of solitude and little distraction.

I had ridden, on occasion, with some of the Centennial cowboys who were still tied to that remote land. They rode horses as wild as the mustangs of the prairie, and had to be expert horsemen—deft enough to catch a hind foot in a small loop of the hard-twist rope while in the saddle. With one foot off the ground, the horses seemed as gentle as Smoke. What a way to ride a horse.

Centennial Valley is far more important to Montana than it has been given credit. The first explorers and trappers crossed the valley and the Continental Divide and made possible a connection to the settlements of the Midwest and Salt Lake. This was the most important road into the gold discoveries at

Grasshopper Creek and Alder Gulch. The opportunities, the climate, and the fertile soil of these valleys became known nationwide. The ruts of the pioneer and toll roads, upon which Grandfather Perrault freighted supplies to these valleys long before River Ranch was born, could still be seen from the range riders' cabin.

Our trip back to the ranch was with equipment needed for cattle drives, and not for frontier freight outfits. By this time, the calf boot on our wagon was empty. But by fall, the tiny calves that rode in the boot in the spring will be heavy critters. We would still have the calf boot when we came back in the fall because ranching depended upon calves coming along anytime throughout the year.

We headed down the road along the north slope of Centennial Valley on toward the ranch, passing the log house with the six children—we still did not see them all. We stopped at a high point on the divide to take a long last look at the valley with its ponds and swamps and birds. This was the scene to fill our thoughts for the long trip home. We turned our horses and headed north along the foot of the bench, following the tracks that the trail herd had passed the day before. We would meet the old pioneer road in a few miles, and then we couldn't lose our way on home.

The little log cabin and the two old folks who lived there were in the front again as we passed. We waved a greeting. We would reach the forks of the Ruby in an hour and be at the Upper Ruby cow camp. It was an easy ride on past Poison Creek. Larkspur was no longer a worry.

At the forks we loaded up all the gear we had left, lit the fire, made a pot of coffee, and nibbled on odds and ends of food the cook was willing to part with. We switched to our favorite horses—Smoke would take me home. The other horses were turned loose and headed down the road toward the ranch. The wagon couldn't make it to the ranch in one day, but as light as it was, could make it in two. We'd camp along the trail somewhere between there and the Ruby River notch, wherever dusk found us. There was no need to hurry and there was a real reluctance to leave that mountain paradise. We were now headed for home at a walk, and each person was with his own thoughts.

Dusk fell when we were within sight of the Caswell place. It was no chore to care for the few horses left. It was so quiet that there seemed to be something wrong. No calves bawled and no cows answered. No old bulls were standing around eyeing the camp, and no cows were roaming around looking for calves.

The fire was a bed of coals. The coffee pot was boiling and the Dutch ovens that had bounced along the rough road were now filled with beans, salt pork, and biscuits for the meal soon to fill the old granite plates. This would be the last supper along this cattle trail until the fall. The tent had been raised and the lantern lit. Now to bed and to dream of the fall gathering, when we would renew our acquaintance with those white-faced cattle we had left on the summer range.

At daylight, we had to get up on our own—there were no cows to bellow out the alarm. There was, though, as most every morning, the yip of coyotes. The horses nibbling their oats, the full coffee cups, and the hotcakes and bacon in the skillets signal breakfast time on the trail. The horses were saddled, the gear was stowed in the wagon, and we were soon on our way to the ranch.

In just the few days it had taken to go from the ranch to the summer range, a great change had come over the valley. Now the cottonwoods were shiny and the limbs were sticky and oozing sap. The round, green pods on the cottonwood limbs would be spreading cotton in no time. The birch had nearly leafed out, though the leaves were still small. The willows were green and all leafed out—the pussy willows of spring.

Drake mallard ducks flew back and forth along the river, but hens were seldom seen: They would be with the little ducks. Magpies and crows chattered and scolded near their newly built nests.

Meadow flowers had begun blooming, and the alfalfa fields were green. Farmers were in the fields with their farm implements, and many plots were black and newly plowed.

The village of Alder had no audience. Doors were back on the Buffalo Hump and we decided that a personal inspection was not necessary. Laurin had no road agents hanging from the trees. The store had not changed; it would look just the same for years into the future. We crossed the river bridge at

Laurin and headed on toward River Ranch. Our horses would be at the feed rack long before the chuck wagon arrived. The horses we turned loose at the forks of the Ruby were nowhere to be seen—they were out on the prairie and would come in for water tomorrow or some other day.

Dining that evening was a time to talk and to relate the old and then the new events along a cattle trail drive. It was also a time to listen to Grandmother relate tales of the trail and the trials across the endless prairies into this valley.

She said, "There was a day, long ago, at the ranch when the old Indian chief and his tribe came to camp at the headgate. He squinted at Grandpa with dim eyes. He said, 'I know you, when you cross the plains, you pee in my face.' "

Montana was Idaho Territory when Grandfather came in early 1860s. It became Montana Territory in 1864, Grandmother made the trip in 1871. There was a settler just here and there in those early days. The valleys had scarcely been scarred by the plow or the harrow. There was yet no barbed wire to account for anything but small plots and few ditches. Deer, elk, and buffalo were everywhere and anywhere. While Grandmother recollected, we could listen and relive the spring trail we had just completed along with those that Grandfather and Father had traveled years ago. Though there was settlement everywhere now in the valley, our cattle drive to summer range had been almost like the first one of Grandfather Magloire Perrault.

part 2

A YEAR AT RIVER RANCH

summer

the fourth of july

The Fourth of July was a special holiday for country folks. It was the first good day of summer to go fishing and the day of the big barn dance. When the barn dance passed, haying at the ranch would soon start.

For the Fourth we dug a block of ice out of the old ice house, filled the ancient icebox in the kitchen with ice, and crushed what was left for the ice cream freezer. We churned and churned and finally the ice cream froze. All we had to do now was hope the fish would bite.

The creek in the meadow was high and crystal clear, which made the big brown trout want to come into it when the river was muddy. A badger-hair fly and grasshopper would taste as good to those trout as the trail-cooked food tasted to me, or as the ice cream would taste as soon as we got back from fishing. When it was almost noon, we had most of a dozen trout hanging on the willow branch. There would be plenty for breakfast in the morning to go along with the hotcakes, ham, bacon, and eggs.

The ice cream that we had packed in ice that morning was now frozen solid and there was no time wasted in licking our bowls clean. Mother spent the rest of the afternoon preparing delicacies for the baskets for the midnight supper at the Fourth of July barn dance.

The barn in which the dance was held had no saddles and no tack. There were no piles of scattered straps that some wild horses had torn up, no lariat ropes or snub ropes hanging on pegs anywhere. The barn was cleaned and the floor where the cows and the horses were kept had even been washed. Yet barns are barns and while the cows and the horses were missing there was no mistaking the smell.

In the gravel yard, our old Model T was joined by Franklins, Dodges, and a Maxwell, just like Jack Benny had. The dancing took place in the barn loft where the summer hay would soon be placed. The holes along the sides of the loft floor had been covered so the dancers would not fall into the mangers below the way the hay did. As the evening wore on, some of the dancers could get a bit limber and they might wind up eating hay in some cow's stall. The loft floor was slick from the hay, needing no wax and no polish. In one corner was a platform about fifteen feet square where the musicians and the square dance caller would be above the dancers.

Ranchers' wives were busy, between visits, with lunches and preparations for the midnight supper. Months of news and the happenings of summer were the gossip of a thousand bees. The ranchers traded information about cattle and horses, and the farmers about crops and prices.

All the ranchers, farmers, and their families were shaved, shined, and dressed in the country garb of the day. Most older men had removed their hats and stood about in groups. They wore colorful shirts and almost all had a kerchief. Sometimes there was a gold nugget, diamond, horseshoe, or other style of pin in the kerchiefs. Many of the men had plain Levi's and western belts with big buckles. Most of the boots were shined as if for church. The ladies wore long gingham dresses of many hues, designs, and patterns, and almost all wore high-button shoes. It was a colorful crowd of ranch and farm families at play on that Fourth of July in the valley of the Ruby.

The young cowboys and the young ladies were something to look at. The young fellows' hats were of most every color and most had wide brims. Hats were shaped with creases, like the flattops of the old-time gunman; some had no dents, but just high crowns. All those young fellows, with their faces scrubbed clean and shaved—those who really were cowboys, those who thought they were cowboys, and those who wanted to be cowboys—reminded me of the little fresh white faces and pink noses of tiny calves.

The young fellows' shirts and kerchiefs with fancy knots, were often silk in the brightest colors. Their jeans were all western with copper rivets, and each pair was worn with a wide belt with a big fancy buckle that was meant to turn heads. Their boots were even shinier than when they bought them. Their walk was definitely western, and great pains were made to leave no doubt. A lot of years, a lot of horses, and a lot of practice would be needed before those walks would be authentic like Father's, Joe's, and Ed's.

Now all this preparation was not lost on the young ladies. They were ready for this July event and then some. They were all beautiful, or at least I thought so. There were brunettes, blonds, and even some redheads. Their hair was done in the most beautiful styles, often with fancy ribbons. They wore earrings along with fancy pins with gems that twinkled like the stars out along the trail. Some had bright ribbons around their ankles that would show beneath the long gown when they walked. Some of the gowns barely missed the floor. The patterns of the dresses, with the ruffles and the lace that set those gowns off, was something to behold.

Whatever the young ladies wore and how they wore it seemed to work wonders. Matrons who were busy with lunches and other necessities for this gala party fidgeted a bit as they stole glances (at every opportunity) at their daughters. Perhaps they were remembering being that age. Their glances were not lost on the young fellows, either. Some of the faces were red, and it was definitely not from sunburn. Some were nervous and shifting from foot to foot. All those young fellows were well aware of the quarry and were nervously awaiting the bell to begin the chase. The sound that would begin the evening gala event should come any minute.

Bullerdick was quite a fiddle player. He was a farmer's farmer, and tonight his gray head and handlebar mustache looked right in tune with the bright red shirt and the blue jeans he wore. No one ever noticed his shoes because his jeans hid most of them, but you always noticed Bullerdick's legs. Though I doubt he ever rode a horse, many young cowboys would have given anything for a pair of legs that looked like Bullerdick's.

Bullerdick had a red bandanna in the pocket of his jeans and a bright red silk kerchief with a fancy knot around his neck. His gray hair, now rather thin, was neatly combed and parted. His wrinkled and weathered face was mostly a huge broad smile. His blue jeans were faded and outlined that pair of barrel-stave legs, which somehow came from following the plow and not from bending around the belly of a horse.

Bullerdick stood on the stage, fiddle in one hand and bow in the other. The square dance caller hopped up on the stage, too. His hat was pushed back and his face was a big red moon sliced with a broad smile that seemed to say, "Get ready for the fun." Then Bullerdick placed the fiddle beneath his chin and drew the bow. The sound was like nectar to bees.

The caller tossed his hat to the back of the stage and his happy face and smile plainly said, "Now the dancing will begin." And it did. "All right, girls and boys, bow to your partner and do-si-do. . . . Now, all join hands and circle to the right . . . allemande left and grand left and right . . . now bow to your corner lady . . . now swing your partner . . . and then prome-nade the hall."

The barn swayed to the time of the fiddle and the tunes that came to life. Knees bent, arms waved, boots clicked the floor, and laughter and joy filled the loft of the barn like the hay that had slickened the floor. About midnight "The Old Missouri Waltz" slowed things down a bit, but by this time the quadrilles, the square dances, and the waltzes had given some reason for the red faces. The self-conscious looks of the young fellows had been replaced with smiles, laughter, and joy. What those faces failed to conceal was that the stalk and the chase would soon take a different twist.

The lunchboxes were taken up to the stage. They would be sold to the highest bidders, and the proceeds would go to some community cause. When the auction was finished, by some miracle, it seemed, the partners who had been close together during the evening had somehow got the right lunches. Some of those lunches did go for rather high prices, I thought. The ribbons, the bows, and the other decorations of those baskets could have something to do with the even-tual winners.

After about an hour, the fiddle wailed again. The floor was soon filled and the caller bowed again and boomed out those intricate instructions to the dancers. Again the barn creaked and swayed to the gyrations of the dancers. As the evening wore on, it was clear that some of those looks and moon-eyes would last more than one night—this might be the beginning for some couples. There would be some sad good-byes at day-light when the dance ended.

Once in a while one of the old tin junkers by the cotton-wood trees belched and groaned like it was time to go on home. July the Fourth was well along the way to the fifth, and it was almost daylight. In a few minutes the sun would replace the need for lights on the old cars. The old flivver bumped, ground, and rattled along the country road to River Ranch in the bright morning sun. Early morning of July 5 had arrived.

haying, snakes, and coyote hunting

One afternoon after the barn dance, I headed for the pasture on old Buster to get the saddle horses for the next day's big ride. Buster was no ordinary horse. He had been quite a bucker in his younger days and had hurt his ankle stepping in a badger hole while chasing horses. Buster had cost us only twenty dollars, so we turned him out in the mud by the swamps. In one summer he was completely cured of any limp.

Buster hated cows as much as Smoke liked them. If you rode him alongside a cow, he would try to bite it. We never took him along on the trail drives or to work cattle. When it came to chasing horses, though, Buster could run all day—there were few wild bands that could shake him. Tomorrow we would corral one of those bands to get the extra horses we needed for haying.

We had several teams that were ranch fixtures. Old Prince, a bay, and gray Shorty, two Percherons, and several others. Prince and Shorty were the two we used to hitch with the mustangs—with or without owners—that we aimed to get from the prairie.

Extra horses were needed for haying because some of ours were generally laid up with injuries or for rest. Sometimes we got horses from a farmer who needed help to tame them so they could be used on his farm.

We caught the band of mustangs almost at Stone Creek, some fifteen miles from the ranch. They had dropped down from timber and were headed for water. There was about thirty in the band—a big bay stud and several yearlings, along with mares and colts. I recognized a couple we had used last summer.

Nowadays these horses are known and protected as wild horses. In the days of this horse roundup, though, they were horses gone wild, whose lineage went back years and whose lives were not spent entirely on the plow and the harrow. These horses were out on the prairie the same as a stray cat or dog that had been abandoned along a country road. We aimed to get some of the wild horses back to the ranch and then back into the harness.

I was on Smoke and Father on Buster when the race began. The wild horses headed straight down the wash. They broke out across the prairie and we pushed them hard into Big Hollow. When they reached the end of the hollow, the wing fence turned them into the corral. When the corral gate closed, we had begun haying.

There was a big black and a big bay in the wild bunch, each six or seven years old. We had never seen them before, and they had a strange brand that we did not recognize. They had either cleaned a farmer up (when a cow or horse out-smarts a cowboy, he is cleaned up) or been abandoned to the prairie.

We roped the bay first. That bay horse had cleaned some-body up, all right. We dropped the rope while it was still tied to his neck and let him loose. When he ran around the corral I looped his front feet. We tied him up, both front feet together and the top hind leg with them. We let him sweat a bit and then haltered him, let him up, and tied him off to Prince. It turned out that he had been broke to lead, so we took him to the barn and stalled him. The black horse was wild, too, but he had a more gentle disposition. He was easy to lead to the barn—tied to Shorty—and to a stall.

Most of the day was gone by the time we caught and gelded the young studs in the band. There were no horses in the bunch that were worth running a brand on. Ranchers who cor-ralled the so-called wild horses for any purpose always gelded the studs. That was the only way, besides shooting them, to keep the numbers down. We could never do that, even though the horses were worthless. We had taken the only horses we would need, and we opened the gate and turned the rest back onto the prairie.

It was cool the next morning when we went to the barn. The two wild horses were definitely not against eating the

A hay stacker like those used in the 1920s on the Perrault Ranch. *Photo courtesy Montana Historical Society, Helena*

good hay. They liked the oats even better. We got the harness ready and got Prince ready, too.

The bay horse found himself tied up collar to collar with Prince. There was a bit in his mouth, a rope around his neck, and blinders on the bridle. I opened the big barn doors and swung out on the neck rope, and Father had the lines. The bay did not walk out of the barn real sedate-like, and when the team got outside and he tried to climb out of the harness and kick, Prince grabbed him by the neck and pulled him down, throwing his weight against the bay and almost knocking him off his feet.

Horses have a great fear of being helpless; when the bay found he was all tangled up he stood real still. It took most of an hour to get the act together again. A couple turns around the wagon and the horses were on the right sides of the tongue. There was some dancing and some running. After four or five miles of this act, Prince and the bay were back in

Although this is not a picture from the Perrault Ranch, the gin pole hay stacker is like the one used on that ranch. *Photo courtesy Montana Historical Society, Helena*

the barn. Those oats must have tasted pretty good. Tomorrow would be the day to really start haying, and that team would be out in the field on a hay mower.

The first swath was far from straight and the corners were a bit ragged. In another day we would get all the odd lines and the corners straightened out.

Oh, we had a lot of runaways, all right—on mowers, wagons, and most all machines. In a runaway, sometimes, the gentle horse could be guided. If the runaway team hit a haystack, the gentle horse would put his head down, but the mustangs would try to go clear through the haystack. When he backed out of that hole he would calm down. Swamps were a great stopper for runaways, but sometimes you had to get pulled out of there. Leaving a horse helpless for a while gives him plenty of time to consider the folly of running away. However, a swamp stop almost always meant a day off to fix up the farm machinery.

Once the hay was cut, the vicious mosquitoes disappeared. When the hay was raked into windrows and picked up to go into the stack, the hawks would swoop down within a few feet of any rig and snatch a field mouse. Then they flew away to their nests or to some fencepost to enjoy the catch. A pair of pheasants had been introduced to the river bottom, and near evening their broods came out. Often there were a hundred pheasants in the field, following any implement in the field to snatch the bugs and beetles. The old cocks hung around the edges of the flocks. Hawks gave the pheasants lots of room.

When we put the wild hay up in the Jones field we rode to work in style. We were the proud owners of a surrey, a fancy carriage with fringe on the top, which had beautiful leather seats and running lights that burned kerosene for use at night. At the day's end we hitched the haying teams to this con-veyance—which belonged nearer the turn of the century—and headed for home.

My sister's girlfriends often visited the ranch. The first night of their stay was generally spent talking and giggling, but even so, early breakfasts were strictly enforced. In sum-mer, if necessary, the first morning of the girls' visits began with a guided tour, from bed directly to the barn—barefoot, of course. The second morning saw the table full, though some of the girls would have nodding heads.

One day the girls came to the hayfield to watch the serious business of haying. We stopped long enough to show them the big fish in the deep hole of the river. It did not take much of a push for them to join the fish. The girls thrashed about in the water and stirred up some food for their new friends, and then we all went back to work.

Hay corrals were always filled with high weeds. The old-fashioned hay rakes with the big curved teeth were scary— and so were the half-broke horses that were hooked to the rake. I mowed the hay, but someone else had to rake it. It paid to be the boss's son, even without wages.

I mowed one of the hay corrals with high weeds, and a long rattlesnake skin turned up in the swath. The snake had shed the skin in the hay corral and he could possibly still be there. Rattlesnakes were serious business in cow country. While they were found in quantity out on the prairie they were almost never found in the damp wild meadows, so I rode over with the hay mower to where Father was raking and spread the news of the big skin. He had just headed for the hay corral to rake the hay himself.

I stopped to watch what happened. Father went around the corral sitting on the rake's seat, just a few inches over the hay weeds and the rake's long curved teeth. He was singing some French song, holding the lines of the team in one hand and a switch in the other. The song stopped suddenly and he floated off the seat when a nervous rattlesnake sounded off inches below his posterior, so comfortably seated on the rake seat.

The Frenchman stood facing the team, he and they just as surprised as the rattlesnake. He still held the lines in one hand and the switch in the other. Then he began to harangue the rattler with a lot of choice French words and a few not-so-choice English words. Although that wasn't enough to cause the snake to expire, he did leave the world in a violent manner once that team got tied to the fence. I made a couple turns around the field and stopped to look over at the hay corral. There was that French fellow back on the rake. The mellow tones of "When You and I Were Young, Maggie" floated across the meadow.

On Saturday night all the horses went in the pasture for a rest, and Sunday morning we went coyote hunting. We had a dog that was supposed to be some kind of greyhound. What that spindly skin-and-bones really was, I sure didn't know, and I doubted anyone else did, either. He was thin as a rail and always made one think he was starving to death—though he ate twice as much as any other dog. We kept that skinny you-don't-know-what dog as our share of the coyote-hunting pack.

A half-dozen cowboys showed up with the rest of the dog pack, some on horses and some in ancient rattling autos. The old spring wagon had a box built on the back, which would hold the dogs. A fancy light team was hooked to the wagon. They were real fast. The seat was tied down so it would not fly off at some critical time.

I was on this seat with Skinner, who was the most comical and the loudest-laughing cowboy in the West. To Skinner, an exciting time was any narrow escape from death connected to a horse.

With the howling hounds in the box on the wagon and a half-dozen outriders, we headed for the prairie to match our wits and our lives against Mr. Coyote. We rolled along the rim of Sand Hollow, and sure enough we soon saw the quarry.

The old coyote couldn't believe his eyes at the spectacle. It only took one second for him to decide that he was in the wrong place at the wrong time, and the chase was on. The out-riders fanned out so the coyote would be kept on the level prairie—where supposedly the buckboard would, with luck, hold together—and Mr. Coyote couldn't get away by running into those sharp little cuts along the rim of Sand Hollow. Any sane and reasonable person would question the whole business of these madmen and that coyote.

Now we had to hang on tight. This was not a race, it was a runaway. With all the yelling and the laughter and with one guy shooting his six-gun, that fancy light team was on the move. Skinner was at the height of his glory, laughing and hanging on with one hand, his feet hooked in the dashboard to keep from flying out onto the prairie.

The fancy team had been in this race before; they needed no guiding—as if any guiding were possible. The team was try-ing to outrun the coyote. We finally got close enough for the hounds to see the coyote, and by some lucky twist of fate, Skinner managed to turn the buckboard around so that the back end, full of hounds, was toward the coyote. We had not even turned upside down, though some of the wheels had been off the ground much of the time.

I pulled the rope with the hand that was not hanging on for dear life. The gate of the dog box dropped and the hounds sprang out and took off. Howls, barks, and whines could be heard in town miles away. Mr. Coyote turned on the steam and headed right back to Sand Hollow.

We got the fancy team stopped and watched the spectacle. With the howling and barking of those mongrel dogs, along with yelling and laughter of the outriders, I marveled that the old coyote did not just lie down and die of fright. He was far too smart for that, though, and he was tough, too.

Mr. Coyote cut back and forth across the little canyons run-ning into Sand Hollow. Sure enough, out jumped a jackrabbit, and he ran back and forth and soon the dogs were running after the rabbit instead of him. Those dogs could have caught the coyote, but running up and down the canyons and the

hills of Sand Hollow after the jackrabbit was another proposition. Well, in a while, one by one the dogs got tired and run-
down, and the rabbit was still running up the hill and waiting
for the hounds to catch up. When the hounds crawled up the
hill he teased them some more. Finally, Mr. Coyote sat on a little hill about a half mile away with a big smile. Tired, happy,
and all in one piece, we all headed back to the ranch.

Coyotes were the outdoors, and when I was younger I
longed to have one to raise. On one of these excursions we
turned up a den. I watched that den from a distance until the
little coyotes began to come out. Then we dug the den out and
I became the proud owner of seven little coyotes. I fed the
pups cornmeal mush and, after about a month, jackrabbits for
dessert. Six of those coyotes never tamed a bit. One, however,
the most beautiful one—Nicodemus—was as tame as any dog.
He did not wag his tail like a dog; it went around and around
in a circle, instead. While he wagged his tale 'round he smiled
with the finest set of hardware I had ever seen. Those canine
teeth were about twice as long as those of the hounds. He
loved to be petted and he would lay his head back and smile
when his back was rubbed.

No matter the begging and the pleading, Mother had held
firm. No coyote was going to get out among her chickens, nor
was he going to have any opportunity to taste any of those
turkey drunks who did not have enough sense to come inside
from a hailstorm. Finally the sad day came when Bassett, the
fur buyer, got Nicodemus and all the other coyotes. Now
Nicodemus was in coyote Happy Hunting Ground.

What did Nicodemus think about that boy, with his sleep-
less nights, who loved him so, and yet would steal him from
his home? And what did he have to say about the fancy lady
who now had his skin for a pretty wrap?

the august circus

Mowing, raking, and stacking hay saw July pass into August. In mid-August we began to look forward to taking a break from haying to see the grand circus the following week.

The Ruby Mountains held many stories and in some places, near timber groves, lots of chokecherries. The Sunday before the circus, we went with a neighbor to the chokecherry groves in Big Dry Canyon. The bushes were especially loaded with fruit that year, and by midafternoon we must have had ten gallons of ripe cherries.

Picnic over, we hiked up the canyon for something to do. Up Big Dry Canyon, high in the Ruby Mountains, was a tiny creek that ran a short way and disappeared into the rocks. Once there was a sawmill by the creek, and as we neared the old and dilapidated cabin two small children ran from it crying, "Daddy, Daddy." Well, the neighbor and Father had a long visit as I looked over the old sawmill. We left, with the neighbor and Father each carrying a jug of Montana cough syrup. The revenuers would never think to look up there, and we would never tell.

The Ruby Mountains had a lost gold mine. Many years ago, Grandfather used to ride the range up to those mountains to visit an old French miner. He would take fresh eggs and other food along to share with his friend. The old miner claimed to have a fabulous mine. He had to have something, because he took the ore to Dillon twenty miles away on the backs of his burros in sacks. One summer the old miner went to Canada and never returned.

For many years the mine and the old miner were forgotten. After Grandfather passed away on one of our trips to the Ruby Mountains, we found a small pile of rocks that was gold ore. It had been propped against a small tree many years before. The burlap sack that held the rocks had rotted almost away, and the tree was bent from the pressure of the sack against it. There *was* a mine somewhere. High up on a ridge, near a small spring, we found a tiny cabin that was fastened together with rawhide strings. The mine was still lost, but we looked for it each time we got near those mountains.

Monday was the day to go to the circus in Dillon. We left early so that we could see the parade, watch the men drive the stakes for the big top, and watch the elephants raise the huge tent.

After noon, the show was ready to begin. Folks came from miles around to buy tickets. The calliope was playing its way to the big top with a following of cages, accoutrements, and animals of this grand circus.

Inside the great tent, we saw the clowns and the trained lions and tigers perform dangerous stunts. We closed our eyes when a fellow put his head in the lion's mouth. Elephants stood on tiny stools, and when their show was over they looked at us with sad, sad eyes and held out their trunks for peanuts. Of all the animals, the well-trained and beautiful horses were the best. They danced and strutted in a show that even our own Buster and Smoke would have enjoyed watching.

Midget couples got married I suppose at least once every show. The midget named Charles played tunes on a small piano, accompanied by another midget who played a violin. The thin man strode around the crowd with a high hat and high-heeled boots. He was most of a head taller than anyone in the audience. The fat lady had a dress with ruffles, which made her look larger than a stack of hay. There was an Indian dressed in buckskin with long braids of black hair. With a handful of clay he would fashion most any animal, which, though drab in color, would defy any flaw in conformation.

Just when we were sure the high-wire performers were about to fall almost a mile to the floor, the clowns appeared. Their great red mouths and purple hair caused eyes to wander from the sure disaster about to happen on the high wire. When all that excitement had passed, on came the cage and the wild man.

The wild man was something to behold. He had long unkempt red hair and his chest looked like the red hide of a big old shaggy buffalo in the wintertime. His red and shaggy beard left no doubt that he was really wild. Even the tops of his toes had red hair. The only place the red hair was missing was the bottom of his feet. The small trunks he wore left little to the imagination. His cage was just like those of the lions and the tigers, bars of iron close together with a huge chain and padlock on the door.

I spent some time inspecting this primeval character and wondering if he could be an ancestor. When Father went over to the cage, both he and the wild man looked carefully at each other and then they both became thoughtful. The smiles and the huge grin of the wild man faded away. The teeth of the wild man, which had looked so white a moment ago, were no longer visible.

Out between the iron bars came a great fist and a red-hair-covered arm. Onlookers immediately drew back in fear. "Hello, Frank," the wild man said. "Hello, Red," my father replied. The show stopped and there was not a sound for a couple of seconds. Then the screams of laughter and glee of the now standing-room-only crowd echoed from around the big top. The wild man, Red, had once been one of Father's hired men. While the crowd looked on in amazement and happiness, the wild man and that French fellow were happily discussing old times at the ranch. P. T. Barnum was not the only showman there that day.

The grand circus had yet another attraction. Years earlier, a circus in Dillon had a group of beautiful Appaloosa horses trained to march and dance to the circus band. The Diamond O Ranch in the Beaverhead Valley had purchased the stallion for a princely sum, but he had gotten away from the ranch, joined the wild horses of the prairie, and had defeated all attempts to capture him. The offspring of that horse and the mustang mares were prized as saddle horses.

Appaloosa horses were native to this region. They were selectively bred by the Nez Percé, who were famous and wealthy in capital—which in those days was horses. Smoke, the prairie horse, had been sired by a circus stud. Now he had my brand, which was recorded in 1874, and was included in the original purchase of land for the frontier ranch. Smoke had first been wild and free on the prairie near the River Ranch.

first storm at river ranch

September always brought a snowstorm followed by huge flocks of water birds flying south. That first taste of winter was cause for everyone and everything to prepare for the cold and freezing winds of December and January.

Early fall days were spent fencing the haystacks, fixing fences, getting the weaner-calf corral in shape, and getting the woodpile ready. When we returned from fall roundup there would be little time for any ranchwork except with the cattle.

One day we were in timber in the Ruby Mountains, high up one of the canyons. The wagon box had been removed, and we had walked most of the way. There was not much of a seat on the hounds (running gears) of a wagon—just the wheels and axles and the fifth wheel and tongue to turn the wagon. The front and rear axles were connected by a pole, called a reach, that could lengthen the wagon according to the length of the poles we were out to collect.

First we had to cut the long, small poles and limb them. About fifty poles make a load, and near noon we were ready to split the team and drag the poles to the wagon for loading. Near dark the wagon was finally loaded and the chain binders securely fastened. We were ready to begin the journey back to the ranch.

Headed down the way was steep, more trail than road. The small green pole tied to the brake was bent almost double by the rope I was hanging on to. The brake shoes were sparking fire from the bits of gravel and rocks thrown in them and rubbing against the iron rims of the wheels. It was a steep and fast ride down the mountain canyon while sprawled on the top of a load of round poles on a bucking wagon. It took only a few minutes to get to Spring Canyon spring, where we stopped in awe and reverence of our good luck to still be in one piece. The team was unhitched and watered, the load binders were checked, and home we went. It was almost twilight and the gentle grade made the ride easier for us and the horses.

Every other day we made the trip for timber in the mountains. Some days were enjoyable, with sun; some days were cold, with the rain and sleet of fall. The pile of timber was a bunch of work and a bunch of cold feet in blustery days. I would have been glad to take those white-faced cattle anytime.

One autumn day I had to take a mare through the valley of the Beaverhead River and across the prairie to the Diamond O. It was shirt-sleeve weather as Buster and I climbed the hill to the edge of the prairie, leading the mare. The mackinaw, scarf, and mittens tied on behind the saddle seemed out of place. The silk stocking stuffed in my hat would come in handy later in winter.

When the mare had been delivered, I was a guest for the noon meal, and I began my twenty-or-so-mile ride back to the ranch in the early afternoon. The sky was clear; there was no wind. Early evening would see us at the ranch.

Soon, though, the air began to get sharper and the sky seemed to be losing its clear blue. A haze quickly began to settle in from the north. Then I saw a dark cloud closing in. There I was, not five miles along the way, with open prairie before me.

At the bottom of Sand Hollow I stopped old Buster and put on the winter clothes no one had thought I would need today. The snow was falling heavily, the flakes driven almost horizontal by the fierce wind. The old stage road was still visible— for now. The solid blanket of snow driven by wind hit us in the face like flakes of ice. I thought there was nothing to worry about, though, because Buster was a range horse and knew the way home to a manger full of hay and a can of oats.

But somewhere on the prairie, the road disappeared and there was not a landmark in sight. The old range horse was lost, too. I walked and led Buster while tiny drifts of snow built up behind the prairie plants. We must have been miles from the road we intended to take.

The storm had blown Buster south before its blast. With years of riding on the prairie I thought I knew every bush, every rock, and every gully, but none of them were to be found in that storm. There were only tiny drifts of snow that told us we must turn into the face of the blast. Sooner or later we would come to the mountains or the end of the prairie and find our way—if we didn't freeze first.

Barbed wire on any prairie is the enemy. Sheep and sheep men had no place upon our prairie. But that stormy day, a sheep fence made an almost-frozen cowboy very happy. We just followed the fence, the snowdrifts showing our direction, and finally hit the breaks at the edge of the prairie, miles off course.

Freezing to death on our favorite prairie was not our fate that day. We forged down the breaks and the slopes into the north wind and finally we hit the old stage road again. It was dark and cold and white with blowing snow. The fierce north wind had still not blown itself out when I opened the corral gate.

Being lost in that storm reminded me of another storm, at another time. It was long ago that I helped Father to outfit the wagon with chains and a long reach between the wheels to haul long logs. The wagon was coupled close together, with the front and rear wheels almost touching, to make it easier to pull to the forest. Once at the forest the long reach was installed and the wheels spread apart to haul the long logs.

The sky had been clear at that early morning hour. Father and the wagon soon disappeared into the canyon as he headed for the timber. The trip meant a long day, almost to dark. About noon the clear sky began to cloud and the temperature dropped. Soon it was twenty below with heavy snow falling. By that time Father would have been somewhere out on the prairie, the team crawling toward the ranch with the long timbers.

Father knew the prairie better than anyone, but we all knew that such a blizzard meant big trouble for anyone, even him. A storm like that forced everyone and all animals to seek the closest shelter. Father would have left the shelter of the woods too long ago to get back before the storm became fierce. He was surely out on that open, treeless prairie. Within the safety of the ranch house, we could only hope and watch through the small windowpanes as they became frosted over and darkness began to fall.

In the storm and in the blinding snow the team was blown off course, just as Buster had been in the early fall storm. The team turned east and south in the face of the blast. They made a big circle on that flat and treeless plain, and by accident Father found that they had crossed their own tracks. He recognized a gravel wash and found the old stage road. On the way back to the ranch he faced the fierce wind, crouching in the shelter of the Christmas trees he cut and tied to the load.

At the ranch house, the lights were all turned up, and near midnight the dogs began to bark. I pulled on warm clothing and raced outside to the wagon. It stopped in front of the house, which was sheltered from the gale and the flying snowflakes.

Santa Claus stepped out from the shelter of the wagon and the Christmas trees. Icicles hung from his face and the front of his heavy coat, and he had a beard of snow. Frost and ice hung from the team and the wagon almost to the ground wherever it had not been scraped off by sagebrush. The harness was frozen stiff. Steam from the nostrils of the horses was like that coming out of a big tea kettle on a hot fire; steam was also rising from the snow melting along the horses' backs. Once in the barn, the ice was chipped off the harness and the team was soon happily munching on hay and oats.

Daylight came early, and the storm passed. It was twenty-five below, and the air had the sparkle of tiny diamonds of ice. Father's face had blue-red frostbite streaks, which he would wear the rest of his life. He was there, safe at the ranch, working outside where the cold of Montana eased the frost of the day before.

fall

county fair

A county fair brought folks from miles around for a once-a-year renewal of acquaintance and catching up time.

Barns, pens, and cages held livestock and other farm animals of every kind and description. There were exhibits for and from everyone, from the smallest children to the oldest farmer or rancher. There were prizes, too. After a couple days of viewing the exhibits and judging them, looking at the ribbons and the prizes, the next event—the rodeo—was ready to begin.

The rodeo was really a spectacle. That was the day for ranchers and hopeful cowboys to get together and tell stories of last year's rodeo. It was the day those cowboys spent their time hoping they wouldn't get bucked off or stomped on. The horses of that show were the mustangs of the prairie near River Ranch.

This year about twenty riders headed up close to the timber. We scattered out and for some twenty miles or so, swept across the prairie. We had most of a hundred wild prairie horses headed for the county fair and the rodeo. Finally, we got them close together and pushed them down Sand Hollow into the lane and on toward town.

The old studs and mares, if they thought they were trapped, would turn and run you down with mouths wide open, kicking and squealing all the while. A cowboy might have been able to ride one of those old horses, but that would be a fight to behold. If he got bucked off he would be a goner. If the old studs got together in a corral, the fight would be even more brutal than out on the open prairie, where the weakest one might sometimes get away. But finally, we got the horses in the country lane; the county fair would have a rodeo.

The rodeo was almost the same as those of today, except that the horses were not trained. Calf roping, steer bulldogging,

Even cow hands get goofy sometimes

wild horse riding, and most anything that could be devised for the wild horses was performed. With untrained horses there was no way to know what would happen. Sometimes the horse would lie down in the chute. Or he might buck, or just run and squeal. Lots of things could happen when a cowboy roped one of those horses and his partner tried to saddle him in the open arena.

One corral held the wild horses and another held the calves for calf roping. Still another corral held the steers with horns for bulldogging. The wild cows were in a small pasture.

The arena around the corrals and chutes was scattered with saddles, bridles, chaps, and all the other paraphernalia for the spectacle soon to come. The riders and ropers and the other folks around the corrals were getting the show together. The pickup men were already mounted and ready to go. The bleachers and the grandstand were filled to over-flowing. The hum of conversation and the yells of the little folks signaled that the show must soon begin. So, to start the show, the big old long-horned bull was squeezed into a chute.

A young fellow got to ride that bull as the chute opened. All the ladies in the audience looked at the huge animal and wondered if that was their son trying to commit suicide. The little folks covered their mouths with their hands, drew in their breath, and wondered if that rider was going to get killed. But they all still wanted to see the bull put on a show. The old bull calmly looked about as the chute doors opened. After much coaxing and a lot of spurring, he went over to the edge of the arena to a patch of green grass and lay down. The rodeo had begun.

Some wild horses bucked, some ran around the arena, and some did nothing that they were supposed to do. The saddle riding was followed by bareback riding. All that rider had to hang on to was the halter rope. Most horses performed as those under the saddle had—until the last one.

The last horse was a big, bald-faced roan that we had used for haying the previous year. He was big and strong and surely could buck if he wanted to. That bald-faced horse walked out of the chute and almost ignored the spurs of the rider, then he lay down. Of course, the rider was off the horse and he still held the halter rope. The crowd got real quiet and waited to see what happened next. "Come on, please get up," begged the rider. The crowd became a screaming, wild and happy bunch of country folks, but the horse still lay quiet in the arena.

Calf roping seemed tame after the horse riding. The prizes were awarded based on the time it took to tie up the calf after he was roped. Gus would have won except he forgot to throw the half hitch after he had the calf tied up, and the calf lucked out.

The wild horse riding contest caused a lot of anxiety and excitement. There was wild encouragement from the audience. It was easy to drop a rope around the wild horse's head. The next step was to get the horse blindfolded and saddled, and to crawl up on top of him as the blindfold came off. Finally one pair of riders managed to catch, saddle, and ride one of the horses across the finish line in front of the screaming crowd.

There was no way to tell who would get the first bottle of milk from a wild cow. One cowboy held the cow with a rope tied off to his saddle horn. His partner tried to squeeze the flying teats and get some milk in a bottle. There was no shortage of cows, and they were as wild as the horses.

I am not sure the first cow had much milk, but there was no question she was not about to part with what there was. To the delight of the audience, that cow bawled and kicked, and butted the cowboy milker. Finally she charged the milker's partner's horse and butted that horse real good. By the time that cow had given up any of that precious milk, another pair of milkers won the contest.

The riders had all drawn straws to see who got to ride the mule. But when I got that slick, no-brand mule in the corral and announced that as long as she was unbranded, I was going to keep her, Father gave me a discourse in both French and English that I would not dare to put on paper. I can also add that some of those epithets were directed at me.

Well, I tied the mule up, branded her, and halter-broke her, always with a gentle horse between us. Then, when the mule was tied in the barn, while I tried to figure what to do next, she would jump from one stall to the other and almost managed to choke to death a couple of times.

One day she decided the hay one of my cows was eating looked good to her. She kicked the cow with both feet. The cow died a short while after that vicious kick. I turned the mule out on the prairie that she came from, and hoped she would go to work on some of the sheep out there.

Innocent, the mule with the white star on her forehead and the one white foot, was in the corral at the county fair again. Somehow she had allowed herself to be driven down the lane and to this pen at the rodeo. The cowboys drew straws to see who would ride Innocent. They put a halter on her. She was well acquainted with halters, but the bucking strap, which went around her belly and was meant for the rider to hang on to, was something else. She had never seen or felt anything like that before. When the strap was tightened up, Innocent resented it. Sticks and planks, together with rodeo paraphernalia and the bucking strap, flew high, wide, and handsome. Cowboys disappeared instantly, to the pleasure of the crowd. Innocent stopped and looked over the wreckage, jumped the fence, and headed back out on the prairie. The rodeo was over for the year.

By then it was midafternoon and the riders, the ropers, the wild cow milkers, and all the other contestants, as well as the audience, were almost worn out. The cottonwood groves of the fairgrounds became the location of picnics and of patching up the wounded. About dusk, the picnics over, the exhibits well discussed, and the laughter—which was directed, along with the good-natured jokes, at the contestants—subsided, the fairgrounds became almost deserted.

The county fair was not over, not by a long shot. Everyone went home to do the chores. Cows must be milked each day and there were other daily chores of farm life which needed to be done. The mechanical monsters of the day belched and coughed their way out of the fairgrounds and headed toward home. Once the chores were done, everyone would be back, ready for some more of the gala event. On into the night, the Ferris wheel would turn and the games of chance would be going full blast as the dance in the pavilion wound up the county fair. Tomorrow the fairgrounds would be quiet as a sleeping turtle.

The dance hall was a big building in a grove of cottonwood trees. The music was not the fiddle of Old Man Bullerdick, but a full-sized orchestra, horns and all, and even a piano. The floor was filled with couples. Outside of the grand march, not many of the old Western square dances and quadrilles took place.

What did go on was very different from the barn dance of the Fourth of July. The fair dance was right in town with a crowd of more than a hundred, coming not only from farms, ranches, and the village nearby but also from far-away towns. That dance crowd was as diverse as Montana could offer in those days.

In the beginning, the dancing was nice and smooth, with couples showing off pretty steps. As the evening wore on though, in twos and threes and fours, those young fellows who did not get too banged up in the rodeo—and some who did— began to dance and make some excursions out into the cotton-woods near the dance hall where the cars were parked. After a bit those fellows would come back laughing and joking. As the night wore on the trips became more frequent and longer, and the limps of those banged up in the rodeo almost disappeared. The laughter and the joking became louder with each trip.

By midnight the noise almost drowned out the orchestra, which was by that time playing faster and louder. Everything stopped for a short break to allow the orchestra to catch its breath, and then the music began again. The break gave enough time to inspect the cottonwoods and to look over the old cars. Thereafter, the boots clicking on the floor and the cheers and laughter almost drowned out the music completely. The building shook and creaked to the point that if you walked outside and watched, you would see sparrows flying hurriedly from the roof to the safety of the cottonwood trees.

In the morning light, you could see that the building had somehow held together. The only evidence of the night before was a couple of the old cars with flat tires and a lot of flat, empty bottles scattered about the cottonwoods. Only a few of the riders were there to follow the mustangs back to the prairie, and some of these fellows were mighty careful to sit real loose in the saddle when their horses moved faster than a walk. These riders were also careful to keep the yells down to the low end and to not talk too loud.

Some riders didn't show up, so we left their horses in the pasture; in a day or two the riders would remember them.We opened the gate and let the wild horses out. The county fair was over for one more year.

stocking up

It was barely daylight as I walked along the creek bank. A few shotgun shells and a bit of luck would mean fat and tasty northern mallards for dinner.

October meant freezing at night, thawing and brightness in the daytime, and trees in fall colors. The cottonwoods were few on the ranch. In earlier times, Grandfather and Mr. Thomas, the neighbor, had shoveled a ditch along the toe of the bench slope. They sat along the ditch when the water began to flow in it. "Perrault," Thomas said, "I am going to plant you some trees." The rancher twisted the ends of cottonwood branches that floated down the ditch, and stuck them in the bank. Those were now huge, tall trees—the only trees on the ranch except those planted around the first cabin home and a couple along the river.

The cottonwoods turn bright yellow, and since they are so few, they are striking that time of year. The river's banks are a jumble of brownish red birch. The birch leaves drop soon after they turn, and the branches turn a pretty red. Wild rosebushes near the fences and the river were yellow and bright red. On some grew bunches of bright red berries, called rose hips. Bright red buffalo berries would be sweetened by frost. A few chokecherry trees had dried berries still on the limbs; their red leaves would be the last to go. The river willows lose almost all of their leaves in the fall.

In the fall the swamps were ringed with brown horseweed; the shaggy heads of tall cattails were about to lose their silky fibers. The cattails stand all winter, getting more and more shaggy with each storm, but by spring their heads will look like the raggedy hides of prairie mustangs. As the willow leaves fall and the cattails and the swamp grasses break down, the muskrat and beaver houses stand out like tepees around the swamps. The ditchlike canals form a roadway all around their houses. Stumps of willows show new teethmarks of beavers, and there are spots in the swamp grass where the muskrats have cut it clean. Mallard and teal ducks float along the canals and the creeks among the beaver and muskrat homes.

Magpies and crows are everywhere. Magpies bob along as they fly, and when they find a tree or a willow near you, they'll light on a branch and scold until you leave. Crows flock and set out sentinels as they looked for spots in the fields. A tangle of brush or a fallen log was a cottontail's nest. Near the bench, the snowshoe rabbits were patches of gray, which would last only a bit longer until they turned white. Then the only color in the snow would be their pink eyes.

I hiked up to the high ground above the swamp, a mesa some thirty feet higher than the meadow. It had a scattering of scraggly sticky sage and hundreds of gopher holes and mounds. There was only a little grass because of the alkali soil. There were no rattlesnakes here, but the gophers were kept in a sort of balance by badgers' appetites and by Nature's summer storms. When a storm hits, the rain floods the gophers out, and the hail kills them. That almost worthless ground was also the favorite land of prairie chickens—my quarry today.

Game was not the only source of meat for Montana ranchers. There was only the ancient icebox for refrigeration at the ranch, so each neighboring rancher took a turn supplying fresh beef for everyone. Nature provided the cold from fall through spring. It was not unusual to see beef covered with a tarp hanging from one of the corral gate caps at any time on a cattle ranch.

When it was our turn to supply the beef, we took a stoneboat—a flat platform on two skids—into the field to get the fat beef we butchered. When we got the beef to the corral we covered it with canvas and then hoisted it up on the gate cap. In a week, in the cool fall weather, we could take it down and cut it up.

When the cattle buyer arrived, we went to the field to inspect the fall animals to be sold. The discussion was all about the cattle quality, weight, and shrinkage, and the market.

Finally the buyer, who had purchased our cattle for several years, got around to price. "Well, Frank," he asked my father, "what do you think those steers are worth?"

"Oh, about ten cents per pound," Father replied.

It was quiet for a minute or so, then the buyer said, "Those are good steers, Frank, and I can pay you about one cent more."

"We can ship tomorrow if we make a deal," Father told him.

At daybreak the gate was opened and the steers were on their way to town and the railroad. Those steers were a year's income and profit, and we carefully hazed them along the road toward the stockyard's corrals.

We rode home in the evening speculating about the weights, the price, and the year's profits, and planning for the year to come—the crops to be planted, the calf crop, and next fall's steers. As we rode along home we watched the north, for it was from there that the storms would soon come and churn up the valley.

Montana, on a ranch, has only two seasons: winter and the rest of the year. By the time of the cattle sale, most of the rest of the year was gone, and now we must wait for the northern lights.

The next morning we went to town early in the old Model T. The train was at the stockyard with the first cattle car already spotted. It was part of the deal that our cattle were the first to be loaded. Another part was that no shrinkage would be charged—the cattle would gain weight overnight in the stockyards.

The scale took about ten head at a time, and the rail car held about thirty. We loaded fast, and by noon all our cattle had been weighed and loaded.

The old steam engine on the train gave a belch and a giant blast of the whistle and then, chugging and sparking, the cars, followed by a caboose, rocked and wove down the grass-covered, wavy rails. The cars swung from side to side as the engine belched black smoke. The caboose looked like a little house chasing a drunk down the track. I saw a teacher and a group of little children watching this show, and imagined that, years later, those children would tell their children about us—the cowboys, the cattle, and that rickety old train.

After the cattle sale, the draft was deposited at the local bank. It was written on school note paper, but passed for a fancy check with numbers in the thousands. When we left the bank we headed for the store—having some money again we could buy the winter supplies and pay the summer accounts.

The long list of supplies included sacks of flour, sugar, beans, salt, cornmeal, and other staples that would last long after winter had passed. When deep winter finally set in it was often days before we could get safely to town. Even then, not much could be carried on a saddle horse. We loaded the old Model T and headed for home.

The old washboard roads shook a few bolts loose with that load. Anyone who drove a Model T in that valley always took along a few wrenches, a chunk of wire, and a pair of pliers. We would make it home, but the time factor was questionable.

We had a big cast-iron kettle, a lot bigger than the old tin bathtub, which was not only usable but much appreciated. You could sit across the corner in that tub—without your knees hitting you in the chin—and wash the most needed parts.

The kettle got many different uses, such as today's: boiling water to scald hogs. When the water boiled it was put into a wooden vat some two feet wide and six feet long. The poor old pig, now dead, was dropped into the boiling water and would, in a few minutes, lose his hair to dishlike scrapers.

When the hogs had been cleaned and dressed, the cutting up would begin. Nothing was wasted—even the hair was saved for plaster binder. Hams and bacons were trimmed. When my uncle came along with the secret recipe, the meat curing began. All the trimmings were rendered and the lard was stored in ceramic crocks. Sausage and other meat to be used fresh had to be cooked and stored in jars to keep it from spoiling. Pickled pigs' feet were considered a delicacy when winter storms were raging.

We put the preserved pork in the root cellar, which had a wall of shelves already nearly full of jam and jelly, chokecherry syrup, and even some canned peaches and other fruit not grown in the valley. There were piles of carrots, turnips, and rutabagas, and a ton or so of spuds.

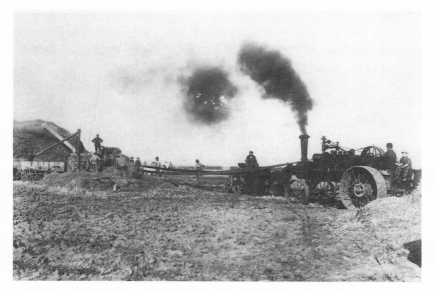

A steam threshing outfit similar to this one was used on Perrault Ranch.
Photo courtesy Montana Historical Society, Helena

The sandy bench soil near the ranch produced the finest
and largest potatoes found anywhere. To harvest them, we
plowed deep furrows alongside the hills, turning the plants up.
Then a close-tined fork was used to shake them loose from the
vines. We could only turn up those that could be picked each
day or the frost would spoil those left in the field. When we
finished the week of potato harvest, our little bit of farmwork
was done for another year.

We traded our labor with a friendly farmer nearby, who cut
our oats and bound them into bundles. To a farmer, thirty or
forty acres of grain is a headache. To our horses those oats
were something else indeed.

The good news about threshing was that it only came once
a year, in the fall. The bad news was that it lasted all winter.
We were the last stop in the valley for the threshing machine.
We did a lot of work and a lot of helping other farmers to get a
little bit of oats threshed every year.

The first threshing machine in the valley had been a steam
outfit. When Father was a young man, Indians on beautiful

Appaloosa horses would come to watch the threshing. When the engineer blew the steam whistle, the horses spooked, travois came apart, and children and goods scattered everywhere. Teams of horses ran away with the wagons and their loads were scattered about the field. More than one farmer recounted the events with a laugh, as if the whole business were a joke.

The second threshing machine, still operating, was powered by a Big Four tractor like those now rusting away out on the prairie. It was a monster. The wheels were most of six feet tall and the rims two feet wide. The motor alone was as big as a Model T. There wasn't much difference in size between the old steam engine and that gasoline-guzzling junkyard, the Big Four tractor. When it came, the Big Four tractor took over the steam engine's stall in the shed, and the poor old steam engine now sat outside along the wall.

It took a lot of expertise to run a Big Four. The anemic machine would get stuck in any small ditch. It was so heavy that almost all the bridges had to be reinforced before it could cross, and even with that precaution, the tractor once managed to drop into the creek through the bridge near town.

Taking the threshing machine from field to field, the farmers would usually detour to the saloon in the nearby town for lunch. Suds at a dime and a sandwich to boot meant a lot of grain got threshed that afternoon. All the farmers, even my own father, left me back by the creek to watch the horses.

Ranchers like us who raised just a little bit of oats for our horses generally stacked the bundles in the fall. When the threshing machine finally came around it would be positioned between the stacks, and the grain bundles would be pitched into its conveyer.

Farmers, who raised a lot of grain, threshed out of the fields and hauled the grain bundles to the threshing machine in wagons. At threshing bees, farmers from all around joined in with their wagons and teams. Several men would pitch bundles from the shocks into the wagons. There were often six or eight such outfits in a crew.

I had to do chores and feed the horses, and I always arrived a couple hours late for the ordeal. I would ride over there on horseback and I got to pitch the heavy bundles into the wagons. I was reminded many times by the farmers how good it was for a young fellow to pitch the bundles, how it made big muscles. I never said anything, but as far as I could tell the only thing it ever did for me was make me tired—the big muscles just ached most of the night.

Sometimes, if a farmer had a good day and a good crop, he would see that I got a dollar or two. He would ask if I liked hunting those big, northern, green-headed mallard ducks. Well, I could hit those big ducks with my Monkey Ward shotgun shells. That was a lot more fun than exercising big muscles. If there was any money left after buying shotgun shells, there was always a need for fishing tackle.

Threshing feasts were found only by hard work and luck. There might be as many as a dozen or so men on the threshing crews at the table. The farm ladies got together to prepare the feasts. Each farm lady would try to outdo all the others when it came her turn to make the food. There was never a delicacy that was overlooked. When the table had been set and the meal begun it was never a question of what was the most delicious or your favorite food, it was a question of how to sample each dish and still have room for the various desserts.

At one of the threshing feasts, when the pumpkin pie with whipped cream was passed around the table, one of the fellows said, "Well, I plumb forgot about the pie. But I am not going to let it get away, or give it up. I'll just smear it on my face."

fall roundup

Late in the summer, Indian summer, we headed for summer range to round up the cattle and bring them back to the ranch for winter. There was no frost at the ranch at night yet, but there would be plenty up in the high country. We would trail along with the chuck wagon until we reached the Ruby River forks and Three Forks cow camp.

There were ruts in the old country road, and when we hit the old toll road they were deeper yet. Moseying along in that shirt-sleeves weather made us all anxious to get along to summer range and the mountains.

First camp of fall roundup was at the Caswell place. The next day we threaded the notch and followed the hillside near the open meadows of Upper Ruby River valley along the river. Along the way we saw some of the high mountains with a cap of snow.

After another night, it was a short run on to Three Forks, but the road was all uphill. That night we fired up the cabin stove, and the horses had pasture. We looked for the doe and her little fawn of spring, and indeed, they came out of the brush along the river as soon as evening fell. Very soon the twilight would be washed with bright stars and the moon. It was hard to stay inside a cabin with a show like that outside.

Just past dawn the next morning, the chuck wagon was leaving the forks. We didn't ride along with it that day, but went on to summer camp on the slopes of Centennial Valley to begin fall roundup.

The sky was full of screaming water birds flying about swamp potholes. They called and talked, their sounds muted by the mellow tones of the great trumpeters.

We rode into the clouds of sage grouse as soon as we hit the hills. Deer stood motionless in the sage, but the fawns were still too small to be seen unless we scared them so that they ran. That evening, in the chill, our old friends the coyotes tuned up and harmonized for the frosty night.

The larkspur along the rim and at Poison Creek was wilted in patches, and the blooms were gone. The chuck wagon would be along in the evening, and then fall roundup would begin in earnest.

September storms had left the Snowcrests with a skirt of white, and the high mountain meadow climax grasses had gone to seed. Patches of willows along the creeks were now bright red. The aspen groves were a bright yellow, and those high up on the mountainsides had already lost most of their leaves. The delicate aspen leaves fell at the first breeze. By the time we left the mountains, the aspen branches would be like tree skeletons.

When we arrived at summer camp, we were greeted by some of the old cows, trail-wise and ready to head for home. All the cattle seemed to be restive and uneasy. Wild range cattle knew when it was time to go to the high summer ranges and they knew when it was time to return to the lower valleys. There were very few late-summer calves, and those we had brought up in the spring were now fat and heavy. Most of the cattle had not yet moved from the high country down to the lower meadows and the flats along the creek beds. The bulls were all still high up: Some would be in the lodgepole thickets and the mountain swamps, and we would find some cows and yearlings with them there.

At dawn we were again greeted with the lowing of the cattle near the cabin. We began the roundup on the highest range and canyons with those cattle that were farthest away to group and push them together, down the slopes toward the valley. As soon as we began to move cattle, some of the old trail-wise cows began to move down the slopes on their own—they knew they were now ready to begin the trail to the ranch.

After riding the hills and the canyons for four or five days, we still had not found the old steer. We had most of the markers in the herd, but no old steer. Markers were easily identified animals who had some color or trait that set them off from the rest so that they were red flags to the cowboy. To leave that high range without the several distinctive markers accounted for could easily have meant the loss of not only the markers but also of others who might have been overlooked. Winter blasts in these high mountains levied their charge without concern to anything or to any animal, and without notice. Since the old steer might not have been alone, we would have to hunt until we could account for him and any others. The lodgepole thickets and the mountain swamps were hard to cover, and they sometimes contained deadly hemlock.

High, open ridges were often the scene of Fourth of July lightning storms in the summer. The steer, or what was left of him, lay high up on one of the bare ridges, burned splotches on his remaining hide. The scattered bones and the clean-picked ribs of his frame told the final chapter of his fate and the power of the summer lightning storm. That old steer was only one of the thousand in this herd of cattle, yet he was an important marker.

Ice was on the spring the next morning. The trail-wise cows were headed home by themselves. They hardly took time to stop and feed as they rambled along the road. Most of the cows did not have to worry about their calves because by now those calves were capable of taking care of themselves. By noon the cattle were strung out far enough ahead to make the turn to the old pioneer road and head down the slope. There were not even a couple hundred head left in the drag.

In the fall, the road was dry, and the alkali dust soon coated the gear and clothes of the cowboys who followed the cattle. We had kerchiefs like those worn at a barn dance, which covered up as much of our faces as we dared. At the alkali stream of that night's camp we slapped our hats along our chaps, took off our shirts—the only wrap needed in that Indian summer—and listened to the old cows call for their calves as the dust settled.

Trail dust was no big deal to us. Some of the dust on the gear and the clothes was already streaked with alkali from the night before. There would be a lot more of that dust on the long trail down the valley and on to the ranch. Once at the ranch, though, the trail dust and the sweat of the horses would soon be lost. That time of year the river was too cold for swimming, but the woodpile would furnish fire for water in the old tin tub in the bunkhouse. Soon the kerchiefs and the alkali-streaked

Frank Perrault's Thoroughbred horse, Topper, stands by as he takes a
Saturday night bath at cow camp in 1950

shirts and jeans would be at the country dances, washed
clean.

During the night the cattle moseyed along and ate. By the
time we left camp in the morning, the lead was near the
horses. The grass was white with snowlike frost and the little
creek had a skim of ice on all the slow spots. There was still
plenty of alkali to streak the dishes, but the trail coffee
smelled and tasted better than ever.

As day broke the coyotes were sounding off. They were
locating all the coyotes in Montana. Their orchestra soon
sounded like many—one or two coyotes on each hill could
make a lot of noise. Sage grouse were flying about close to
camp, inspecting us. If they were not bothered, and you could

Opposite: Frank Perrault on his Thoroughbred mare Lady on the
range in 1940

walk slowly enough, you could get close enough to touch them. As they squatted upon the ground they looked like tiny sagebrush bushes.

Smoke and I moved along beside the meandering line of cattle. We were on our way to the winter pasture, the river meadows and oxbows. The cattle seemed as unready to leave this paradise of mountain and meadow as I was. However, we had to get busy and stir up the lazy cattle and those not yet ready to go.

The lead was past the forks, and when we got there we worked back slowly. Tonight would find some cattle near Ice Creek. The chuck wagon was sneaking up on the evening camp. Smoke and I rode past it to help the cowboys on the drag. By dark tonight all the herd would be on past the camp.

At Three Forks we put the horses in the pasture and gave them a feed of oats. Then we ate a trail snack ourselves. It was already getting dark and we were ready to hit the hay. We were anxious, but not ready to hurry to get the cattle home to the ranch. Trailing herds of cattle was a job of just following the herd—as long as they knew the way. Even without the old steer this herd knew the way, and they would get to the ranch in good time.

As we began to ride to the lead of the herd the next morning, some of the cattle were again far ahead on their own. When we reached the lead, Smoke and I were already close to that night's camp. Tonight we would be looking into the Ruby Valley.

The Caswell place was the last trail camp this year. The tent was pitched and the fire was a bed of coals, with the coffee pot alongside. It was a pioneer coffee pot, battered, black, sooty, and good-smelling. Odors gave away the evening meal. It would be ham, beans, and hot biscuits just now baking in the Dutch ovens. There was some strawberry jam for biscuits, and cups were brimming with coffee made from good spring water.

When the meal was finished, the dishes were washed by the cowboys. The evening chill began to settle, and it got quiet. We were ready for the sack, yet hesitant to go to bed. Here the stars shone brightly even though the sky was still not dark. An old cow bawled for her calf next door. This was the place coyotes sang close by, and ducks and geese barely missed the tent as they flew over. As I lay in my bedroll for a few minutes before sleep came, I could still hear outdoor sounds in the air.

We rose in the light of a new day, before the sun was up, and our breath hung in the air as we ate what would be the last breakfast on the trail this year. The Dutch ovens would soon be stored away for another winter, to await the spring. Breakfast was just getting settled as I jogged along on my horse. The taste of bacon and coffee lingered on as we wound our way along the long, slender, scattered line of moving cattle. Frost rimmed the grass and the river willows.

We turned our horses down the country road to meet the drag of the cattle herd. The lead of the herd was near Silver Spring; headed home, they will hurry the herd on to the ranch. Along toward the early evening the herd headed down the big hill in a scattered line to head into the open ranch gate and the meadows of River Ranch. It will take most of another day for the last of the herd and the trail dust to reach the ranch and settle.

There were fences along most of the lane and the cattle were following them, looking for a bite of grass here and there. It was almost dusk. This was the longest leg along the cattle trail—we would be in the saddle long after dark.

The ranch folks were out in front of the house and were watching the herd wend its way across the face of the big hill along the road near the ranch. Some rushed out and opened the gate into the field. There were several miles of cattle in this trail herd, and while those folks were able to see only a mile or so of the cattle, that was a great sight for them. The trail-wise cows knew they were almost home, and they quickened their pace as they headed for the open gate and the meadow.

I rode at a slow pace toward Mother and the other folks. I could see the question on their faces—most were ready to break into tears. Almost all together they asked, "Where is the steer?" It was difficult and saddening to tell his story, even though his not being at the head of the cattle had really done so already.

Overnight the cattle quieted and the cows and calves all mothered up. Now we split off the herd for ownerships, animals to be sold, and calves to be weaned. We had been with the cattle for a long time and we knew most of them. Individual markings, manners, and traits of a cow and her calf bound the pairs together. Brands then established ownership.

Splitting the herd to ownerships begins with the pairing of the cows and their calves, some of which may not be branded. Once pointed out, a good cow pony will follow a cow or calf and sometimes give a calf a little nudge with his nose. In no time at all that cow or calf or both are out on the edge of the herd where the outriders push them to the corner.

When we finished working the cattle, we were a few short. We had some from other ranches, which had strayed onto our summer range. We would wean the other ranchers' calves and feed them along with ours until they came to get them. Someday we would be sure to get ours back. It could, however, be next year for either or both of us. Ranching in the great open ranges meant there was lots of time to visit with other ranchers and to straighten out the strays.

The ranges we ran our cows on were very big, open, remote spaces. No one wanted to trade those ranges for anything. It would be foolish to string barbed wire—as in the valley—just to keep a few cows from straying. Should that happen, the roundups, the camps along the trail, and big cow country would be gone forever. Then Montana, the life of cattle men, cowboys, and cows would also be lost. A ranch on the river would have no meaning and no purpose.

a matched team of sorrels

The cattle roundup, with its days of bright sunshine and the fall nip in the air, made me remember a different kind of roundup in a Montana Indian summer when I was a boy. One late October day, Father and I were bouncing along the country road in the Blacktail Deer Creek country of Beaverhead County, a few miles north of the Continental Divide, along a road with a pole jack fence. The pole jack fence is built with three poles on the outside and a rub pole on the inside spiked to the crossed jack posts. That fence was many miles long and belonged to the P & O Ranch, which had several thousand cattle and many sheep. We followed it in a southerly direction and then turned up a narrow gravel road along Blacktail Deer Creek.

We drove through the canyon and into a basin that opened beneath the mountains. Near the meadow's edge, we stopped in front of a single-story cabin with walls of logs a foot thick, notched at the corners and stacked to the eaves. A short path led to the few plank steps and onto a narrow porch across the front of the house. A four-paned window was framed in each of the walls. Some wildflowers had bloomed and gone to seed on the sod roof, and there was a good crop of brown, ragged weeds up there, too. A pitcher pump with a rusty handle stood in the corner of the porch, with a bucket on a rough-hewn and weather-beaten low bench along the porch railing. This cabin had once been a homesteader's, but was now a line camp on the P & O's huge ranching outfit.

We were there because my father had a great urge to own a pair of matched sorrel Belgian draft horses. This was the horse roundup that the P & O held each fall, and perhaps such a team could be found here. A horse roundup at this big outfit was an event no cowboy could afford to miss.

River Ranch buildings, about 1945

The round corral was about two hundred feet across. No homesteader built this corral—no homesteader ever had the livestock to fill it. The corral was made of posts, about eight feet apart and eight feet high, and poles about eight inches apart, and it had gates that opened into smaller corrals and into the meadow along a pole wing fence. There were almost a hundred horses in the corral: Many were riding horses, some were draft horses, and there were a lot of colts, too.

There were about a dozen horse wranglers. The fellows were working cowboys with a selection of Western apparel in the best of styles: colorful, bright kerchiefs around their necks and bright shirts mostly tucked into Levi's, with blue and red bandannas hanging out of the back pockets. Many shirt pockets held a sack of Bull Durham with the tag hanging out and waving as the cowboys worked. All had hats, from those that were seeing their first horse roundup to those that looked like the horses had run over them. Most all of the cowboys had chaps; some were leather bat wing with fancy emblems, some were much like leather leggings, and some were either black or white sheep wool. Of course all the cowboys had spurs, some with rowels almost two inches across and with many teeth, others were the long shank Mexican kind with the star rowels, and some fancy with polished silver.

The wranglers' horses stood still saddled near the wing fence outside the corral; each saddle had a slicker tied on behind and a rope fastened near the swells. Some of these horses were experienced with roundups; some were first-timers. One was a bronc: I knew because the rider had to tie up a foot to get off. No one walked anywhere close behind any of those horses.

Rod was the ramrod on that P & O outfit. He was a huge man who rode a big bay horse with four white stockings and a blaze. Rod had a wide-brimmed hat that covered a head of shaggy gray hair. The corners of his eyes had crow's-feet from years of squinting into the sun and facing fierce Montana storms. He wore a blue shirt, and the kerchief about his neck was black silk with a fancy knot and a beautiful silver clasp. There was no Bull Durham in his shirt pocket. His chaps were smooth leather with narrow bats, and his jeans, which were worn smooth, had crept up above his high-heeled boots. A pair of polished silver spurs with long shanks and big rowels took my eye.

Rod was surveying the roundup as Father and I approached, but he gracefully dismounted and came toward us. Father was six foot two, but he was thin, and as Rod stood close I saw he was half a foot higher and almost twice as big. He shook hands with Father and in a deep booming voice that came from somewhere down in his boots, he said, "Hello." Then Rod turned to me and my hand got lost in that huge fist. When he shook my hand and I wondered if I would get it back, my eyes were level with his huge silver belt buckle, which was a couple inches higher than the laces on his chaps. Rod said, "Son, let's go take a look at those horses."

Rod opened the gate into the corral. Several of the wranglers were looking the horses over, and we joined them. It took Father and Rod almost an hour to look over the horses and discuss the merits and lineage of each one. There was, however, no matched team of sorrels, and no other team would do.

It was near evening—the air was getting sharp and the shadows were getting long. We were guests, who must stay for the evening meal. We headed up the narrow path for the log house. The wranglers had cared for their horses and were all coming, too. While I pumped the pitcher pump, Father washed up, and then I skimmed my face and hands with the cold water. Rod took off his chaps, but not his spurs. They clanked on the floor as he moved about and washed up.

There was only one room inside. The floor was made from pine boards and had been scrubbed clean. The ceiling had log rafters and more pine boards with knotholes. I looked up, expecting to see dirt from the roof fall through those holes, but none came.

In the front corner of the room sat a large cast-iron range with a big oven and two warming ovens overhead. A neat pile of wood was stacked against one end. The stove was blue hot and the oven door was open.

The wranglers straggled in after they had washed up and sat back on their heels along the log walls. There were no chairs and no table except a small one near the range, which was stacked with dishes and silverware. Most of the graniteware cups had been taken and filled as the wranglers went by the two huge graniteware coffee pots that sat on the edge of the range. Nothing could compete with the aroma of that old-time coffee in the great outdoors of Montana, or with the truly Western cowboys who held those cups.

Near the range was a butcher block about three feet square, like those in the local butcher shops around the valley towns. A hindquarter of beef sat on the block and a heavy knife about two feet long beside it.

The cook was a large, round-bellied fellow with a white apron covering his blue jeans and a bright red shirt with a black silk kerchief. A red bandanna hung out of his hip pocket. His face was round and bright red not only from his natural complexion, but also from the hot stove over which he worked. His hair was thin and gray like Rod's.

I found a place along the log wall and sat back on my heels just as those wranglers had done. Father was on one side of me and one of the wranglers on the other. Only the clinking of Rod's spurs broke the quiet as he moved about filling coffee cups. I wondered if Rod wore his spurs to bed. Some of the cowboys had roll-your-own smokes going, and now and then one would blow a smoke ring.

The cook picked up the big knife and expertly sliced the beef into thick steaks. With one hand he cast salt across the hot stove and with the other he flipped a steak onto it. The steak sizzled for a minute or two while he readied another. With a long fork he picked up the sizzling meat, again cast some salt, and flipped the meat over onto the uncooked side. Then he reached into the oven, picked up a big baked spud, and sliced it open. Into that spud went a hunk of butter and onto the steak went another.

Since we were guests here on the fall roundup, Rod handed me the first plate and Father the next one. A boy's eyes are always bigger than his stomach, but I was a boy whose stomach was going to get the test. There was no way to send any of that food back because that would have shown great disrespect to the cook and to Rod. So I went to work cutting bites from the thick steak and nibbling on the spud. Some of the fellows were on their second helping while I was getting fuller and fuller. Finally I managed to stand up and take my distended belly over to the dishpan and wash the plate, knife, and fork.

Both Father and I went over to Rod and again shook his hand. "Come and see us again, son," Rod said.

We walked out the door, across the porch and down the few steps to the path, and climbed into the flivver. Then we headed down the narrow gravel road into the canyon. I stretched out (being very careful of that over-full stomach) upon the hard seats of the old car. I forgot all about that matched team of sorrels, my eyes closed, and for me that horse roundup was over.

crossroads ranch

River Ranch was a crossroads in the Ruby Valley. As soon as the cattle came from the summer ranges there were always buyers, guests, and others at the ranch. Cowboys passed with strays, or with cattle or horses, or sometimes just rode over to visit. The bunkhouse was most always full and the stalls of the barn were filled with strange horses. The small field off the corrals was seldom empty.

They were noisy and happy crowds of people. All the range and the ranch happenings were discussed at length. Many of the events were accompanied with great bursts of laughter and good-natured ribbing. Woe be it to the poor, unlucky fellow who got bucked off in front of company, or in front of anyone who could testify he saw it. The aches and the pains the horses caused and the accidents of ranching were just an inconvenience. Fortunately, no one ever got killed. Often, though, a cowboy would have a built-in limp or a twisted leg, but even those seemed to still fit a horse pretty good. A plain broken leg or arm was just a minor hazard from working with those half-broke horses. All real cowboys had a limp or a hitch somewhere.

I cared for the horses. It made no difference who they belonged to, all horses got the same treatment: good hay and a bucket of oats. Unless I knew the horse, I never walked in the stall alongside him. Some of them were just plain dangerous, but some of the cowboys who sat at our table would ride no others.

There were always ranch chores to do daily. Besides feeding and caring for the horses—and sometimes the studs required more care than any baby—there was the barn to clean, the cows to milk each morning and evening, and the dogs and cats to feed with fresh milk. We had all read and heard over and over again about the famous Swiss dairymen and their wonderful Swiss cows. Personally, I never could figure out why anyone would want to bring any of those cows over here anyway. One of ours would always wait till I got a couple inches of milk in the bucket and then expertly put her foot in the bucket. If she missed the bucket, she always kicked the stool out from under me. Sitting on a cow barn floor is not recommended. Father would never let anyone hit an animal, but it didn't hurt him not to know that some of those nasty old cows got milked directly by the calves. That way the buckets did not get dirty, either.

We filled a big shallow pan with the fresh milk and the dogs and the cats would eat together, though each kept a wary eye on the other. The dogs got to lick the pan and the cats used the extra bit of time to disappear so the dogs could not catch them. One of the cats would always run up the stairs to the loft, likely hoping to add a mouse for dessert. The other, a big old black cat, would run behind the horses and then to the barn door.

When the door was pushed open, Blackie would leisurely poke his head and body outside, leaving his tail hanging inside while he surveyed the landscape to be sure all was clear. Then he would slowly pull his tail out past the jamb and go outside. One evening Father closed the door too fast. The cat was outside, but most of his tail was still inside the barn. The nerves in that tail were tied directly to the cat's voice. He squalled, yowled, and spit, all the while held fast. All his pawing and scratching had no effect on his fast-caught tail. Finally, Father got the door opened along with a few French words that left no doubt the cat's tail was in the wrong place at the wrong time.

The next morning the cat was back for breakfast. His tail had a bend sharper than any country lane and he was very careful how he moved it. Thereafter, old Broken Tail would survey the outside from the inside and then make one big leap to safety.

Despite any of our cowboy injuries, we always made it to breakfast on time. In the mornings our big ranch table was filled to overflowing. The plates of hotcakes, ham and bacon, eggs, cereal, fried spuds, and other delicacies were loaded so heavily that it seemed to be more like a hotel than a ranch table.

That fall, Mother was the happiest cook in the whole world. We installed a huge, cast-iron Home Comfort kitchen range that Father bought and that made a full wagon load to be hauled from the rail station. That gray granite giant, with the hot water reservoir and the big firebox, was great for Mother, but it sure caused me to have to haul a lot of wood and pump a lot of water.

I determined to get even by dressing in front of the oven. The tea kettle and coffee pot always sat upon that giant, steaming away, often singing a song as the steam curled from their long spouts. The tea kettle had only a small hole left in the spout because of the mineral deposits of the hard water from the well. The coffee pot never got empty, even though it held only ten or twelve cups of coffee. At some of the ranch meals this regular pot was joined by one as big as a bucket. The cowboys would help themselves and it was certain they were a hungry bunch. The griddle was most of two feet across, and the batter would fill a bucket. Still there was room on that giant stovetop for large cast-iron skillets, which always seemed to be filled with steaks, chops, or ham and bacon.

Although I had to pump the water and cut the wood to run the cast-iron monster, there was seldom a time when I had to do the huge pile of dirty dishes. Instead I would always hear the clicking of high boot heels on the kitchen floor and see the rolled-up sleeves of some of those cowboys. Generally, the dishwasher would tie on a dish towel apron or a flour sack— that advertised the village merchant's brand of fine wheat flour. When he turned around, his big belt buckle would look like a gold or a silver plate above the strings.

Sometimes ranch meals lasted for hours at a time. Cooking, eating, and dishwashing all went on together with the hum of conversation and laughter. It was a good thing that the old cellar had a bunch of apples and even more spuds and vegetables, along with shelves full of preserves.

Those were the days when towns and villages were one day's drive apart for a team of horses hitched to a wagon. Many of the folks who crossed the ranch threshold did so purposely to visit and often just to break the remoteness and loneliness of ranch and country life. Stops between ranches, towns, and the few villages were well known, and the stops were a regular part of the itinerary of the travelers. The doors of the ranch house were never locked. It was no surprise to have a cowboy we had never seen before spend the night at the ranch and show up for breakfast. These folks were accepted just the same as our oldest friends.

Often in the fall we would stop whatever we were doing and help those who were driving cattle or horses. After that we would return and if there was any of the day left we would start our own work. The next day often began exactly the same way. I would have to help Mother peel a bucketful of spuds. "Don't worry, son," she would say, "somebody will come along and eat every one of them." And it most often happened that I would have to peel some more for the next breakfast. That magnificent pile of cast iron with the double warming oven, the big water reservoir, and the huge oven emblazoned with "Home Comfort" rarely cooled down.

Although some of the days in the fall seemed as if we were running a hotel, those days were tame compared to the times when the house was full of ranch folks. Old Bassett the fur buyer drove up in his Model T, came in without knocking, and announced himself. Bassett was from Kentucky, a shade of Daniel Boone himself. No one could mistake Bassett, with his big handlebar mustache. How old he was could only be guessed at, he was just Bassett. Most of the wrinkles on his face were around his eyes and mouth from the happy smile he constantly wore. He wore a cap like those of the railroad engineers, black with an emblem in the front that had long ago faded mostly away. His neck was covered with a red bandanna. His deerskin vest covered his always blue shirt, and his blue jeans were stuffed into the tops of his high-laced boots. When he opened the door, the words "Hello, folks" floated in with his hearty laugh, which was the signal that tonight would be an unforgettable evening.

Someone would go out to Bassett's old Model T truck and bring in his banjo. Bassett had a wide repertoire of jokes and songs, including his own compositions of the South. They were happy, comical, and sad, and often drew copious tears, either from laughter or from heartrending sadness, depending wholly upon Bassett's whim. Here were we, all from the West and then there was Bassett, from the South. From the moment the banjo spoke, the West and the South were one.

Bassett picked a mean banjo, which he accompanied with his mellow baritone voice and a hearty laugh. He made songs like "Old Black Joe" come to life. At first it was only Bassett singing, but soon everyone joined in singing the southern songs. We all knew the western cowboy dirges and the fate of "Little Joe the Wrangler."

Those were long and wondrous evenings filled with the greatest and happiest memories. This is the Montana I remember from my youth.

As a youngster, along with Father, I visited Bassett's home on the edge of the Cabbage Patch in Dillon. From his front porch you could see little log cabins scattered about without regard to street or law. Those who lived in and visited the cabins came and went mostly at night when the few lights in town were generally out. Red lanterns scattered here and there did not give much light anyhow.

To the south, the Cabbage Patch was cut off by a huge pile of wheels, axles, and every imaginable part that was once original equipment on some ancient flivver. Once in a while there would be an aluminum pot or pan, bright like a pair of eyes, or a bright bit of brass that looked like gold, scattered throughout the pile of junk.

Alongside the interesting pile of ancient automobile bones that had been lost, broken, or shaken loose by the rutted washboard roads and country lanes stood the very first mechanical misfit. The wheels were wooden spokes, of course, with bicycle-sized tires. The little square box on the back was about the same size as I was high, maybe four feet square, and a few inches deep. Viewed from the front, that wood and metal contraption had a brass flange all around the radiator. The radiator had several rag patches, which must have helped to keep some of the water inside. I thought it would have been a good idea to take along a bucket, just in case. The windshield glass was mostly gone, but the brass frame still shone bright gold in spots. The crank hung down below the radiator like a calf's tail.

While I was engrossed in a close inspection of this antique, Father and Bassett came out to look for a cogwheel that was hiding in the junk pile.

"Mr. Bassett, does this thing still run?" I asked.

"No, son, that was my first truck, in fact my first automobile after I gave up my bicycle. It used to work just dandy but it took a lot of tires on those rough roads. When a tire blew out I was never sure whether it was a tire or some other part of the rig that exploded." Bassett's eyes twinkled and he boomed out his great laugh.

In those days of outdoor plumbing, Bassett had come up with a capital idea. In fact, the little house in the corner of the lot was most luxurious for the time. The door fit so tight the snow could not blow inside. It was a fully equipped three-holer with two Monkey Ward catalogs. You didn't even have to use those slick, hard, colored pages. The queen's throne had a nice soft fur band all around. The day I visited this outdoor mansion it was warm, but that fur must have been awful nice in a Montana blizzard.

winter

holidays

All range cattle were trailed from summer pastures. They were sorted out and sold to herds for the year to come. Cattle buyers thinned out; most went to other climes. Cowboys who had been trailing cattle and horses almost finished their fall work. Nearly all stray cattle of summer ranges were found and were settled into their rightful homes for winter. Sometimes the Home Comfort giant in the kitchen needed only a couple stokes of wood. Visits from ranchers who strayed from their own ranges began to thin out.

Thanksgiving Day was a family day, and relatives and friends came from far and near. Some stayed for a day or two, maybe taking the occasion to hunt ducks and prairie chickens. No one was allowed to kill the deer from the meadows, but there were thousands of jackrabbits. It was great sport to hunt those rabbits that were almost white this time of year. They lived along the edges of the benches and in the ravines.

We raised a few turkeys; they foraged in summertime. We fed them a bit of oats in winter and they fed us on holidays. Raising turkeys outdoors in Montana is an experience. They nested in the orchard and along ditch banks in heavy cover, and when their eggs hatched there were some twenty or thirty all together; a few old hens, a couple old gobblers, and the young chicks.

When a Montana summer cloudburst came along everyone and everything else ran for cover, but the turkeys just stayed out in the storm and looked wise. Hailstones hit some of them in the head, and then they ran around like drunks. Some of them did not recover too well, and that always kept the flock down to the right size. Come Thanksgiving, one of those gobblers no longer strutted his stuff—he was topped off with pumpkin pie and whipped cream.

Montana storms that start winter come most every Thanksgiving time. They are not gentle rains and they have no hail. The storms blow cold winter wind and dark days, and the siren of winter wails. When the storms leave there is a scattering of snow banks here and there on the lee sides of brush and along ditch banks. Open fields are wiped clean by the heavy winds that come with the storm. Then the sky clears and the air turns sharp.

Prairie chickens flourished in the dry brush bench edges. Flocks might be as large as twenty or thirty. Mallard and teal ducks flew in wedges as they cruised the open water of the creek that never froze.

Great hawks soared about the meadows watching for a careless victim that would make a tasty meal. Crows made raucous noise in flocks of half a hundred and they set out their sentinels, in the open fields. Magpies bobbed about the willows of the river and scolded everyone, even the cows, as they reached for the dry stalks of summer timothy.

With a clear sky and a warning of winter in the air, Santa Claus was foremost in our minds. There would be little free time after Christmas, for that would be another phase of cattle ranching. Pastures would be short in hayfields and meadows. The lowing of the hungry cattle told us that soon we would need to attack the haystack we had built in the summer.

A trip to Montana's big city, Butte, was only a day or two away. We made the yearly trip to buy our modest presents and some winter clothing not available in country stores. Of course, there were other sights in that big city that any country boy might want to see.

Sandstone rocks were heated for a day or two in the oven to keep feet warm on the trip. We had to install side curtains in the old Model T to keep the biggest blasts of winter somewhat at bay.

Early in the morning of the big day we poured hot water on the motor to warm it up. The team, Old Prince and Shorty, were hitched to the front of the car and it was put in gear. The rear tires scraped along the gravel as the horses pulled it along, and finally they began to turn. With a loud bang, the old car belched into action. We barely managed to keep the team from running away. I had a feeling that Prince and Shorty could run as fast as that bunch of iron and horsehair if we used the startling bang to get them going.

After all this exercise we were ready to start the trip. There was no dependable antifreeze and it was always a game of how much of the radiator to cover or uncover. When the radiator was steaming it was boiling; when it wasn't, it was freezing. The Fish Creek bench was a giant washboard and it took sheer luck to get across that gravel road without losing part of the old Model T.

Once across the Fish Creek bench washboards, the road through a canyon to the crest of the Continental Divide was where you could look down on the city of Butte. It took all the oomph the venerable Model T could produce to get there. Once over the divide the road went down a steep hill, then over the flats, and on to Butte.

We left Mother at a store where the windows were filled with the most wonderful displays of goods, and parked the flivver a couple blocks away from Broadway on a street lined with small cottages. The front windows of the cottages were large for such small buildings, and each had a flower box with frozen, distorted blooms on spindly, leafless stalks.

As we headed back toward Broadway, the painted ladies sitting in those front windows tapped on the glass ever so enticingly. They were coifed in fancy styles with sparkling jewels in their hair and bright silver lockets on chains around their necks. Their blouses revealed far more than those of the most daring of the young ladies at a barn dance. Their cheeks were bright red like barn paint, and their lips were crimson. The fair skin below their chins looked like the downy heads of the meadow timothy. But we always walked on by.

Butte was high and cold, with narrow streets and old buildings. Almost every other building was a saloon. The restaurants were exciting, and the fancy stores, with more merchandise in each than in the whole of a small town, were impressive to a country boy.

Walker's Bar, which was a full block long, never closed. The entrance was on Broadway, almost in the center of town. The double doors were always swinging as men went in and out. Father held the door open so I could see inside the bar. Kids were not allowed inside, nor were women.

Along the inside wall the green-cloth-covered tables were piled with silver dollars in stacks sometimes a foot or more high. The card dealers had black visors, bright armbands, and a black vest. In front of each was a stack of silver dollars and stacks of colored chips and playing cards.

Men standing at the bar—there were no barstools—would toss coins on the sawdust floor for the swamper. Thousands of bottles stood on the shelves behind the bar, which was covered with glasses of beer and whiskey. Foaming mugs of beer slid back and forth, spilling foam. Whiskey bottles and shot glasses stood in clusters. The bartenders wore fancy striped shirts, black vests, and black sleeve covers to their elbows. Most had handlebar mustaches and long sideburns; some sported huge diamond stick pins in their colorful ties, and some wore gold rings with diamonds as big as robins' eggs.

There was a haze of smoke from pipes, cigars, and cigarettes. Considering the host of men in that huge saloon it was remarkably quiet; there was only a low hum of conversation and now and then a burst of laughter. This was Prohibition in Butte, Montana.

Small groups of miners stood on the street corners, and if you watched them for a while you would see some of them cough and spit as if they had a bad cold. This was miners' consumption. As I passed the groups I sometimes heard a miner call it miners' con.

Some of the men were thin and bent, and some were crippled. Looking at the miners, thinking about their mines and the price they paid to run them, made the half-broke horses we rode seem tame indeed. The impressions left by the miners— of their sacrifices to stay alive in that cold and windy town, of shacks and buildings on a barren, rocky hill surrounded by monstrous piles of dirt and stone shoveled from the innards of the earth—made us all want to go home as soon as possible.

On the way home from Butte we seldom got to the divide before dark. To get there took some time because the flivver had to be backed up some of the steep hills to go forward: The gas in the tank would not run to the motor when the front end got too high.

Once on the divide we could get turned around and look at the lights on Butte Hill. Then we headed down the canyon toward the Fish Creek bench by the flickering lights of our rattling wreck. Of course, we had to keep our fingers crossed that in this cold dark night one of the hard, bicycle-sized tires would not explode. Ranch and home danced before our eyes, looking better all the time.

It took a day or two to settle the excitement and heal the bumps of the shopping tour to Butte. The best cure was the old shotgun. A stalk of prairie chickens in the Jones field worked wonders along with the big old northern mallards that flew over the creek. There could be some feasts that Nature would provide if those old Monkey Ward shotgun shells were aimed just right. Of course, the prime beef of a two-year-old Hereford would furnish the muscle needed to attack the haystack we built in summer.

I could go out to the woodpile and spend some time stacking up fuel for the Home Comfort giant. That did not look nearly as good as hitching up Smoke and cruising the six or seven miles into town to get the paper. Father was just as good a Republican as old Doc Heller, the barber, and he would find some good political news in that paper.

In the early days of ranching, almost at the exact time wood needed to be chopped, some other rancher, often with a friend or two, would show up. There was always enough fire to make coffee, fry steak, or make hotcakes with ham, bacon, and eggs if they stayed over.

Christmas Day began early and we carefully opened our packages. No one took the chance that there would be new wrapping the next year. Contents of the packages were always some article we needed to wear or a modest gift that would last and last. The Home Comfort, that handsome kitchen range, roared loudly enough to almost melt the frost on the kitchen windows.

storms, chores, and radio static

After our trip to the city, winter set in for good. That year a big storm moved in while I was in the barn. When I came out, just past noon, the sun was a yellow disk that I could barely see through the haze. From the north a huge cloud of black moved closer and closer. The temperature had dropped at least fifty degrees in the last hour, and it was almost dark at the ranch. The wind was blowing so hard I had to lean against it to keep my feet. Blowing snow and sand stung my face. I hurried to the house before the storm turned into a whiteout. If I didn't make it, I could get lost in the two hundred feet between the barn and the house.

Once inside we listened to the house creaking in the blasting winds and lit the lamps as if it were night. The windows on the north were frosted over like they were painted. Storm winds whistled and sang along the eaves. Though it was only twenty below, it would surely drop another ten or fifteen degrees when the wind stopped, the sky cleared, and the storm lost its fury.

Two days after the storm began, the wind ceased, the sky cleared, and the temperature dropped to forty-five below. It was bitterly cold. The cattle came out of the brush lowing; and plaintive looks told us it was time to start hauling hay.

We harnessed the team and hooked them to the hay wagon. Their winter coats were so heavy the collars barely fit. Clouds of steam from the horses' nostrils formed icicles around their mouths.

Choppers' mitts with heavy woolen mittens inside and heavy clothing with a mackinaw jacket were barely enough to keep us warm in the arctic weather. Pitchfork handles were wooden icicles that would not be warm until summer. As we left the haystack with a heavy load, the steel wagon wheels rolling over the hard snow made a screeching and screaming sound that could be heard for miles. The cattle knew that sound was their dinner bell, and they came running and bawling from every corner to follow the wagon.

Cold feet and hands warmed as the cattle scattered out among the shocks of hay that we had thrown off the wagon. The cattle were dependent upon us and we well knew we were dependent upon them. Watching the cows and the few small winter calves picking at the hay we threw off the wagon was part of the fun of ranching.

The cold didn't seem to bother either the cattle or the horses as long as they were properly fed and had good shelter and, most important, open water. The swamps in many places on the ranch were fed with springs that never froze, even in the coldest weather. While open water was one of the most valuable things that any rancher could hope for, it had some disadvantages. In many places ice was thick enough to carry cattle and good enough to skate on. Near the springs the swamp grass almost stayed green all winter. Once in a while, a cow would go out on the ice to reach the green grass, venture too far out, and fall into the water. The water would seem warm, compared to the air, and only very seldom would the critter even try to get out. Sometimes the mud in the swamp would make it impossible for any animal to get out of the swamp and away from the ice edges. Of course, the water was not really warm, and if left there longer than overnight, the unfortunate cow would chill and die.

When we fed the cattle, we went around to the swamps to see if we had any winter swimmers. We carried a rope to put around the animal's neck to pull it out. Sometimes we pulled them, bucking and bawling, for a half mile or more to a small corral and protected shed near a river oxbow. Pulling them out of the water was not good enough, because when the cold wind hit their wet hide, the cow would just turn around and go back to what felt like a warm-water swim. We always left the swimmers in the shed overnight until they dried out and got warm again. We pulled out more than one during the winter.

One dark February day we were expecting some calves to come along any time, and we went to check on the heifers. We fed the cattle in a river oxbow that is enclosed with thick, high brush. It was cold and we rode there bareback on the horses because that was a warm way to travel on a cold day—walking over a hundred yards was not for cowboys.

When we fed the cattle we scattered hay first and then cleaned the wagon of seeds. We added a sack of oats to the seeds and leaves and scattered that along the way for the birds, particularly for the prairie chickens and pheasants. Prairie chickens would not eat in captivity, but they had no aversion to eating the same food out in the open with the cattle's hay.

As we went back past the piles we had thrown off the wagon, we saw that we were not only a cow outfit, we were in the chicken business. Birds of every kind were among the cattle: tiny wrens, prairie chickens, pheasants, crows, and scolding magpies. The big hawks flew leisurely around the old oxbow because they had found out a long time before that rabbits and mice also came to the feast. As soon as we left, the deer came out of the brush where they were hiding.

In the late afternoon, on our way back past the spot, we were greeted with a different scene. The cattle were still scrounging around for some tidbit that had been missed, the birds were mostly in the shelter of the brush, and the deer had disappeared. The heifers were standing around; one just became a proud mother. The new-to-the-world little fellow was up; a few falling snowflakes just bounced off him. He was shaky, as are all brand-new calves, but he had already nursed and we knew that Nature had another success. There was no question that the little fellow had it made.

We rode slowly and carefully through the cattle. When we got close to the river we heard a noise in the brush. We stopped dead still and kept the horses quiet, when suddenly a few startled steers stampeded toward the river. There was no way to tell what had scared them or why they were on a race toward the mostly ice-covered river. We just jumped off the horses and headed for the river to get ahead of the steers—to get between them and the river. While we were pawing our way through the brush we caught glimpses of the steers heading out onto the ice. When the first steer got almost to the center of the river there was a blast like a rifle shot as the ice cracked.

We could only watch as first one and then the next and then another, and finally ten steers went through the ice into sure death in the swift river. We hazed the rest of the steers a long way away from the river, climbed back on the horses, and returned to the house with heavy hearts.

The next day, the storm was finally over. The sky cleared to a point that it seemed to almost disappear. This was a cold snap, but it was late in the year and would not last like the cold of deep winter. The days were noticeably longer and the lamps were not needed so early in the evening.

Ranchers anxiously awaited February. The days were longer, the storms not so fierce, and they did not stay so long. February storms seemed to know that it was time to go back north for another year. The Milky Way got really milky, and shafts of colored lights reached throughout the sky. The northern lights portended the end of winter, and they played across the sky in a glorious display of color. Winter would then become a memory—and not a bit too soon.

Where the river cut an oxbow next to the meadow, the pond it left was most of ten feet deep and a hundred yards long. A small inlet remained in the old river channel, and the pond was always full of water. The pond was rimmed on all but the meadow side with brush, reeds, and cattails. This cover was the favorite nesting place for ducks and the other meadow and swamp birds. The brush was full of magpies, crows, and black-birds who built nests there. In the summer there were dozens of turtles, frogs, toads, and water skippers and other bugs in the pond. There were also a lot of brightly colored water snakes around the pond, but never a rattlesnake. In the winter the pond was great for skating—the ice got two or more feet thick.

The skating was very good between snowstorms. After a snowstorm, we had to scrape the snow off and then dam the outlet so the pond would flood. In a day or two we would be skating again—until the next snowstorm.

One winter day we cut some of that ice to fill the ice house. During the summer we depended on the ice from that pond for filling the ancient icebox in the kitchen, for freezing ice cream, and for making cold drinks. The ice had to be cut into blocks and hauled to the ice house near the ranch buildings.

The ice saw was about an eighth of an inch thick, long and heavy. It looked like a wide metal strip with a row of shark's teeth nearly two inches long. It was amazing how fast that saw could cut ice. Even with all the work of pulling the saw, we could not keep our feet warm while we stood on the frozen pond. We cut the blocks about two feet wide, two feet thick, and about four feet long. A wagon, with the box in place, had been backed to the edge of the pond. Then up the plank ramp from the pond went the ice blocks, hooked to the ice tongs and a rope pulled by the team.

The ice house was the old log homestead cabin with a dirt floor and a dirt roof. About a foot of sawdust was spread on the floor. When the ice had been stacked almost to the ceiling, there would be about a foot of room left around the sides and a couple feet over the top. The spaces were filled with sawdust.

Filling the ice house was a hard and heavy job, and a cold one, too. It took more than a week to get the work finished. Working with cold and aching feet was not all bad news, though, because we all dreamed about summer coming, which helped to warm things up and hurried up the ice saw.

Soon would come time to lose the overshoes, and the clothesline at the house wouldn't look like it was hung with dead men. Heavy woolen underwear, frozen stiff, would be traded for summer shorts. Fishing and ice cream were only a few days ahead.

Every Montana winter had storms, but they did not levy all their might every day. When the north blizzards blew, the old ranch house shook, and the wind made music around the eaves. That whine was Nature's special Montana music.

There was, however, other music for a ranch like ours. In the winter, the battery of the old flivver rested in the living room of the house to keep it from freezing. I made a neat box to hide the battery under the low table that held the Atwater Kent wireless radio and its big tall speaker. This wireless radio filled many hours with wonder for my inquisitive young mind.

When the blizzards blew, the radio crackled with static. If that noise had gone along with the hay wagon it would have made even the cows forget about their empty bellies. We soon learned that such music as that static was not only drowning out the music we wanted to hear, it wore out the old flivver's battery in a hurry. Then we had to hitch up the team and wagon and go to town to get the battery charged. Fortunately, there was electricity only seven miles away.

We also twisted the tail of the old Edison phonograph, which played thick, big records. We heard Harry Lauder sing, "It is nice to get up in the morning when the snow is snowing and it is musty overhead, but it is nicer to lay in bed." We could listen to "Alexander's Ragtime Band" and "When You and I Were Young, Maggie." Maybe it was one of those evenings that my father learned to sing that song to the rattlesnake in the hay corral.

When the blizzards wore themselves out and gave up their attempt to drive us to some other clime, the sky cleared. Then the sun barely peeked over the hills between Baldy and Old Baldy mountains, and the thermometer often read forty-five below or lower. Winter days drifted into winter nights, and the stage was set for the wireless Atwater Kent. From Salt Lake City, miles away, came the wonderful music.

As long as we dared, and sometimes till the old flivver battery gave up, we listened to the music. There were no interruptions, not even a singing commercial. At times the music stopped and we were introduced to our kind of comedians, Amos and Andy, Bob Burns the Hillbilly, and Will Rogers, the cowboy with the rope. There were others who came alive on the wireless from many miles away.

We had other forms of entertainment, too. Each book of the *Tarzan* and the apes series, and there were several, would last a few days. The tropics and the rain forest would help to warm you up, even if it was forty below outside. Then there were role models like Hopalong Cassidy and the Virginian in print. We had Hoot Gibson and Tom Mix, too, real cowboys.

Of course, when we could afford to, we went to the movie house in town now and then to see if Will Rogers would spin his rope better than we could. Hoot Gibson and Tom Mix could really ride their beautiful horses. Will Rogers could too, but he could also spin his rope and make fun of politicians; Hoot Gibson and Tom Mix did not do that.

Radio static, as you can see, was not all bad news. Yet even with books and an occasional trip to the movie house in town, the fascination of the wireless Atwater Kent never dimmed. When the Atwater Kent came through, when the old flivver battery held up, evenings in a paradise of Montana snow and stars seemed to last forever.

spring

chinook

In March there were warm days—that is, for Montana—and some cold and windy days. There were still a few snowbanks in the fields. Everyone and everything was looking ahead to the first warm spring days and the green grass that came with them.

The sky was hazy and the wind was howling steadily from the west. Snowbanks were melting before my eyes. The day before had been just above freezing, and the frost of the night before had turned to slippery ice by evening. Today it seemed colder and there was water everywhere. Even the air was wet. It was almost, but not quite, raining. It was several degrees above freezing and yet the air was so heavy with moisture that it was not possible to keep warm. The cattle and the horses had all sought the shelter of the brush from the hard, cold wind. There was not a bird flying, not even the ducks. This was a genuine Montana chinook.

The next morning there was not a patch of snow anywhere except on the high mountains. Puddles of water and mud filled the fields. Along the river the ducks were in flocks headed north in the clear sky. The frost that had heaved the ranch roads was gone; in its place was mud and chuck holes. We had to be careful with the wagon or the roads would get torn up so bad we would get stuck. We scattered enough hay to last two days so that the wind could dry the roads and fields before we had to feed again. Cattle and horses were muddy nearly to their knees. Soon the sun would come out warm, the early plants would green up, and the willows would start to get shiny and soon their leaves would begin to form.

The first sure signs of spring were the dandelions. Those first tender green leaves were the first vegetables of the year.

It was such a treat, after the long cold winter, to have a fresh vegetable. There were only the small town general stores to supply the staples—forget about the trimmings. A country store that stocked a head of lettuce between September and May could not be found in the Ruby Valley. There were plenty of beans, flour, and nuts and bolts, but few delicacies. Ranching is a game of survival; the delicacies of green vegetables in the wintertime were never considered necessary.

Dandelion greens were good only until the plants flowered, but then the blooms made delicious wine. When that time came, the lamb's-quarter greens took over along the ditch banks. It was more than a month before any of the garden vegetables could be planted. Meanwhile, the ranch house windowsills were lined with low boxes filled with tiny green plants that would be planted in the garden as soon as hard frost was gone. Frost in Montana could come at any time; snow for the Fourth of July was not uncommon. On many clear, cold summer nights the water was turned on in the garden to protect against a possible frost. It was only safe to plant a few seeds in the ground before June.

The snow, warm winds, and rain, with brief intervals of sun and a few clear days, was our fate at that time of year. The cattle were already prospecting the sunny sides of the brush patches for signs of grass. Near the edges of the warm creek and the swamps, a green tinge had taken over the drab colors of the fading winter. The marsh grasses and reeds were greening up, and white shoots stuck up through the spring snow. The cattails wore shaggy coats on broken and bent-over stalks. New cattail stalks were pushing up all over the waterlogged swamp edges.

The swamps were filled with singing blackbirds, and tiny wrens seemed glued to cattail stalks. Pairs of mallard ducks floated along the river oxbows and the ponds. In a month they would float out of the reeds with a tow of tiny ducklings. Snipes flew around the soggy meadows near the swamps, blue herons stood on one foot in the riffles of the river and the creek, and kingfishers sat on the branches of the willows that hung over the water and watched for fish. Meadowlarks sat on most every post, singing their spring songs. Big swamp hawks flew low over the meadows, looking for mice and gophers. An occasional coyote was seen near the old stage road in the field, because that was where the gophers first came out in the spring.

The cattle were beginning to desert the hay shocks we threw out for them to look for new green grass. The prairie was just beginning to show the green tinge of the first grass, and in just a few days those range cattle would be looking over the fence at climax grass.

The Montana chinook had driven winter away. It was spring.

springtime

In spring, the meadows were a lake of water. Snow was melting in the mountains and the riverbank was overflowing with muddy water. The spring flood was a foot deep over most of the meadows, where Nature left a rich coat of silt.

Where the bench gently sloped to the meadows, about a hundred acres of land would be tilled and planted as soon as the mud in the fields dried out. Most of the tilled land was planted to oats for the horses, then a couple of acres were planted to spuds and the rest were restored to timothy and clover with a cover crop of alfalfa.

The orchard had a dozen apple trees, and though the summers were short, almost every year there were a couple barrels of apples to store for winter. The garden near the orchard had fertile soil and yielded a ton of vegetables. Now the peas, lettuce, and radishes were beginning to show green shoots. In another week the tomato, cabbage, cucumber, and pumpkin starts in the boxes on the windowsills of the house would be ready to plant. The currant bushes were almost leafed out. Strawberries and crabapples would go together to make jam and jelly, and wild fruits like chokecherries and gooseberries would be preserved, too.

It was late June, and I found that there were no pressing things to be done. Haying would not begin until after the Fourth of July. There was always fence to patch, but tomorrow would be time enough for that. I could slip away and go fishing, but the water was too high and muddy and the fish were too hard to catch when it was like that.

Both Belgian mares had colts, and when we went into the hayfields the colts would have to stay behind in the corral. I decided to educate one of the colts today. I slipped a rope over the sorrel's head—he was confused about what this was all about. His eyes went wide and he reared so high that he almost fell over backward. As the rope paced out he raced around the corral and managed to get all tangled up. He wound up with mother standing on the rope. It was hard for him to breathe with the rope tight about his neck. He backed off a bit and calmed down. I leaned against the mare and she stepped off the rope. I walked over to the colt and stroked his neck. He was not afraid, yet he knew full well he was not free, and he was wary of what would come next. Then I flipped the rope over his nose; completely bewildered, he stood and watched me. After a while I gave the rope a tug and he tugged back. We felt each other out awhile, and then he made a run to get away. When I snubbed the rope, the colt was pulled up short and he flipped around. We played this game until he started to sweat, then I eased off and the colt went over to his mother. Almost before he knew what had happened, I tied his halter and rope to his mother. Leading the mare around the corral taught the colt to lead. Mother had provided another lesson for her offspring.

My father, Ed Davis, and Joe Redfern were fine horsemen and cowboys. Father rode his own horse to summer range when he was six years old. Ed Davis rode the meanest and toughest horses to a standstill. Joe Redfern trailed cattle from Texas to Montana three different times on range mustangs, and was a legend of a horseman.

When we worked the cattle earlier in the fall, Joe went along as a rep for his outfit, Reid Ranch. Joe looked over the horses in the corral, he chose a black mare. We rarely used her because a rattlesnake bit her a while back, and she could only be trusted in a few areas on the range where there was no threat of snakes. She was one lucky horse because she had not been bitten in the face, which saved her from losing an eye. No one could rope off of the mare—she would just go crazy.

Range horses on the prairie often suffer snake bites. Sometimes when the horse hears the snake, it runs wildly away and then gets curious and comes back to smell the snake. That was a sure way to get bitten in the face and lose an eye. A one-eyed horse was almost useless. When you spent a lifetime in the outdoors, you felt sorry even for a worthless horse.

Frank Perrault on his Thoroughbred mare Lady in the mid-1950s

As Joe saddled the black mare, a couple of the other riders came over to tell him about the mare and her dismal record. They suggested that since we were just going to be cutting out steers, he wouldn't even need the hard-twist rope he was looping up to put on the black mare's saddle. Joe said nothing, but went ahead and stepped up into the saddle and headed for the

field. I learned to say nothing in a situation like this, so I just
watched and waited for the action to start.

Ed Davis hobbled over to me and said, "I'd give a lot to ride
with you fellows today. There will be some fun and I can't be
there." Ed's horse, Joe, was in the corral, but Ed could no
longer ride. I could only step into the stirrup and mount up,
but all the while I thought about Ed Davis and the memories
of his salad days. I turned my horse and rode over to Joe
Redfern.

I followed Joe into the field full of cattle, where he began to
uncoil his rope. With a flip of his wrist he dropped a loop over
the horns of the biggest bull in the herd. Then he tied the
rope fast to the saddle horn and placed the reins across his
lap. He reached into his shirt pocket and pulled out the Bull
Durham and proceeded to roll a smoke. A big bull weighed
2,000 pounds; the horse, about 1,000. The mare, who had
bucked everyone every time she could find an excuse, was
only about a foot off the ground and dug in real good. A good
rider learned to compensate for the difference, and sometimes the horse was almost lying down as it pulled on the
rope. The old bull pulled the rope so tight that you could have
played music on that string if you had a fiddle bow. Joe got
the smoke rolled and lighted, and without even touching
those reins he just leaned over a bit. The mare also moved
and the rope slacked off. Joe rode over and without a word—
while for some unknown reason, the bull stood stock still—
lifted off the rope.

So far Joe Redfern had not said a word. There was no other
action going on—everyone was standing still or sitting on their
horses, taking in the show. Joe rode over to me and said,
"Come on, son, I'll show you how to do it."

That is what it was like working cattle with Joe or my
father. Their horses knew exactly what they should do and
always wanted to do it. Neither Father nor Joe seemed to use
the reins. While Joe never said more than a short sentence at
any time, my father harangued cows in both French and
English with words and gestures that only the outdoors could
handle. When Father or Joe got up there, the horse knew he
could buck but did not want to. Perhaps the horse knew deep
down it would not do any good to try. I learned a lot from

those two fellows, and there is no argument, we rode and drove the best horses in the valley.

Hooking up the mare Tanya to the Frazier Breaking Cart to go to town was quite a production. I remember as a youngster looking out the ranch window at my parents headed for town in that two-wheeled rig. I recall that my sister and I spent a lot of time watching out the window for the cart to return. About dark, Tanya, the cart, and our folks would show up. By that time Tanya was tired enough that she would actually stand still for Mother to take packages out of the cart.

Once when Mother returned home, my sister was standing on the landing wearing a beautiful hat. It had a wide brim and a woven strawlike crown and was decorated with apple and cherry blossoms and tiny red apples and cherries. The hat had pink, white, and blue ribbons that hung almost to the wearer's waist. Such a hat would surely grace any belle's head and fit most any costume. The wonderful hat made most any cowboy romantic. It was so beautiful it would make a cowboy forget about his horse.

"Where did you get that hat? Go put it back in the trunk," Mother said at first, but finally when we begged enough for the story of the hat, she softened up. She smiled and I imagined she was sorting out the memories the hat awakened.

"Well, long ago your dad rode uptown on a bronco," she began. I had never known Dad to ride anything else. "The boys got together and went to Dillon to a horse sale. When the night wore on I finally became afraid of all the accidents that could happen with your dad on that bronco. I was frantic. Almost at daylight, the door opened and your father woozed into the house carrying that hat. No one could put that bronco he was riding in the stall at the livery stable, so they called over to Dillon and the boys came back. He rode that horse on home carrying that hat from town. That hat saved your father—and that time it was not his horse."

River Ranch life was a life of the great outdoors. It was a life filled with horses that we loved and white-faced Herefords. It was a life of riding cow ponies over prairies and mountains in Nature's paradise, and hearing the coyote's call or the hoot of the owl. Ranch life was about lying in the comforts of your old woolen blankets as ice formed on the creek.

In the bright sun of early morning, meadowlarks sang out along the ruts of the old country roads. Plowing, harrowing, and threshing were great endeavors, but those deeds couldn't take the place of fine cows, calves, and cow ponies. A field of grain is beautiful, but it cannot take the place of waving climax grass and wildflowers as far as the eye can see.

Cow ponies had to have shoes to travel the country roads and the prairie. If the horses were not gentle—and a few of them weren't—and if we could find a few dollars to spare, we took them to old-time blacksmith Bobby Simpson in Sheridan. Bobby was near eighty and had most likely shod horses before he could walk. When we tied the wild horses to the hitchrack in front of his shop, Bobby came out of the shop and looked them over. He retired to the shop to take a nip out of his bottle of moonshine. His comment was always the same: "It's not that a man drinks a little whiskey, it's generally that he doesn't drink enough." That said, Bobby took another healthy swig, which would go along with most of a quart of that "cough syrup" each day.

He would not allow anyone in his small blacksmith shop when he shod those horses. Honestly, some of those horses would not be safe to be around unless they were hog-tied. Well, there were some dandy knotholes in the rough board siding of the shop, which were as good as a reserved seat at the circus.

Bobby led the horse inside and dropped the halter rope next to the anvil. He got the forge hot, then picked up a rasp that was most of two feet long, walked around the horse and picked up a front foot. The horse was surprised that he dared to touch even a front foot. The horse soon recovered from the shock, slammed his foot down in authority, and spun around to kick old Bobby. Somehow, Bobby had the halter rope in one hand and when the rasp in the other hand hit the hind end of the horse it sounded like a clap of thunder.

In about an hour, Bobby came outside leading the horse, which was proudly wearing his brand-new shoes, his first set of iron ones. With the newly shod horse tied to the hitchrack outside the shop, it was then time to fulfill that quota of a quart a day. The other horses could just wait a while and wonder what a new pair of shoes would be like.

part 3
DEPRESSION RANCHING

crash of change

Doc Heller's barber shop in Twin Bridges, just a stone's throw from where Captain Lewis camped along the Beaverhead River, was the town's principal center of information, conversation, and discussion of current events in the fall of 1929. Doc was a staunch Republican, which always made for many lively political arguments in the Democratic state of Montana. When the arguments got too hot, Doc could always end them by the observation that the legislature must pass two bills. Quiet would prevail and any newcomer would wait to hear about the two bills. Doc would say, "The first bill would be to go home. Most important, the second bill would be to mind your own business." Looking back all those years I see that he gave good advice, which is worth practicing today.

A young fellow who sat and listened till the political arguments wore down was rewarded with the most up-to-date news of small-town events. Especially about the good women and the bad women: who they were, what they did, and how they did it. Discussion often turned to younger beauties of my own age. Then, if you had time to listen, you soon found out not only about their good looks but also about most everything else. It never looked like a smart move to get roped into those discussions.

Sometimes the conversations got around to farming and ranching, especially in the fall. Information about prices and profits, ranchers and farmers and their outfits, and the crops to be harvested were all important to this valley. The prospects of what kind of winter we would have and the grass of the next spring were important topics especially to country folk.

Ranchers and farmers were individuals who preferred no interference. They wanted to outwit Mother Nature, the prices, and all else, and do everything on their own terms. As long as these hardy folks were left alone they were happy—some in prosperity and riches and some in poverty.

Today, the several fellows in the barber shop were quiet, even Doc himself. Not a word was spoken—the shop had never been this quiet before. You could even hear the razor scrape the beard of the fellow in the chair. The door swung open and all eyes turned to the fellow who was entering the shop. He threw what was left of his hat in the corner next to the spittoon. The fellow was gray-haired and his face was wrinkled like a shrunken apple. His eyes were sunk back in his head and the lids seemed almost shut. His bib overalls were faded and had almost as many patches as original cloth. The elbows of his shirt exposed skin and the collar was frayed into pieces.

He sunk into a chair and said, "I've got six bits left for a shave and a haircut." It was quiet except for the scraping on the face of the fellow in the chair. "Sit there and take it easy," Doc finally said, "you don't need the six bits." Everyone looked out the window, and there outside in the street was the man's sheep outfit. Wagons, sheep, and a herder with the dogs: The street was full. He only had six bits left and his outfit out in the street in front of the barber shop, and across the street was the First National Bank, which would take it all.

Then all talk, in slow and measured tones, turned to the crash. Sheep, always the most consistent money makers with the wool in the spring and the lambs in the fall, had dropped from near thirty to about five dollars. There was no market for cattle at all. The fall checks from livestock sales, which we needed to pay off the operating expenses of the summer, were sure to be too small to pay even the interest on the mortgage, let alone other expenses.

The banks in the valley were mostly country banks owned by substantial ranchers and farmers. However, some were speculative ventures, as in many small towns in Montana; often, those banks were sadly undercapitalized with portfolios of shaky loans. The real question was, how long could any country bank hold on? Could any of them weather the storm? Would the money in their vaults just disappear the way a storm fades away? How many suppliers, farm and ranch machinery dealers, and general stores, which fed and subsidized agricultural folks, would stay afloat?

The Montana we knew had never faced a bedrock economy before, not here in the headwaters valley. The fellows in the barber shop who were so quiet that day were no doubt contemplating their own chances, too.

I was relieved to get my hair cut and to step out into the fresh air. I was saddened to watch the herder move his sheep along the village street past the First National Bank, their new owner. I made my way to the old flivver and reflected silently upon this West called Montana.

This was not the Montana we held so dear, yet the summer had been fair. We had hay and pasture. We made enough to clear ourselves of debt, and River Ranch would last yet another year.

after the crash

The great financial crash of 1929 had gone past like a Montana blizzard, and we were ready for a new year.

Spring was something else, something new. The chinook of late March lasted for most of a week, and the melted snow stood in every depression, streamed off every gully to the fields, and finally ran into the river. All the snow was gone, almost to the tops of the highest mountains, and the mud was knee deep everywhere except on the prairie gravel bars.

Somehow we had to get the stock out of the fields, but we had no place to take them. The nights were clear as a bell and freezing cold. Days often clouded over with no sun; nothing grew and nothing bloomed. Late that Montana spring we managed to turn out on the edge of the prairie, finally away from the muddy fields. We fed what was left of the hay to the stock on the edge of the prairie more than a month later than ever before. When the hay ran out there was still no grass. Cattle bawled and followed the wagon, making no effort to go out on the prairie to look for grass.

On that brown prairie, even the gophers who generally came out right behind the snowbanks were nowhere to be found. We had never been able to keep the cattle from trying to push out on that prairie in the spring. When we ran out of hay we pushed the cattle over to Sand Hollow, where some of the ravines and sags in the prairie had old grass and where damp soil had the beginnings of the new grass. We came off the prairie with the branded cattle near mid-June and made ready to trail to the summer range with the hungry cattle at least two weeks later than usual.

Shorty, old Joe, and Prince, the oldest horses on the ranch, had been retired from hard ranchwork. Shorty had developed ring bones on both front ankles, which hurt and made him lame if he worked hard. Prince was just old. They all got along fine in the good pasture with a bite of oats now and then.

Prince, as horses went, was an old, old horse. Father told of going to sleep next to a haystack in the summertime as a young man with his head on the ribs of the colt Prince. Now Prince was ailing and going downhill fast. He was confined to the best pasture and fed oats every time he would eat them. It was a long time since Prince had done any work.

He stood by the pasture gate with oats in the battered pan half eaten by the gophers and birds. He was gaunt, his ribs easily counted beneath the once-glistening bay hide. The skin hung loosely about his frame and his eyes were dim and sad. We had to leave for the summer range early the next day, and there was little we could do but to fill the pan with oats. Like the old steer, Prince was a constant in our lives, but he was an even stronger presence because he was always in or near the corral. Only a few days ago Prince had hung his head over the fence and nickered as we went about the chores. We turned away from the pasture gate and the pan of oats and looked toward the edge of the prairie bench, where tomorrow we would be with the cattle.

From the ranch we headed along the prairie bench and up the big hill with the trail herd. We stopped at all the usual trail camps. The springs and the creeks were all noticeably short. The restive cattle scattered widely, looking for grass. The cows were more protective of their calves, as though they felt somehow the short grass would not still the hunger of the calves, most of which were too young to eat grass yet anyway. We rode the horses far more than usual to gather the cattle and to urge the herd on toward the mountains and the meadows, which had yet to show the green of spring.

This summer range was not the joyous trail of the years gone by. Trail dust was thicker and the deeply rutted roads had not been repaired by a county out of money. The ruts meant little to the chuck wagon lumbering and lurching along and they meant nothing to the horses we were riding; they were just another sign of the hard times.

Sure, we had the same outfit, and a few of the same fine cattle, and fine horses. We camped at the same places and ate the same good food, but the cattle were restless. The bawling never seemed to stop. The cattle were always hungry. They hurried along looking for grass that was not there. Each rancher and each farmer along the trail had a tale of lamentation. The farther we went, the more concerned we all became, and the more I could feel that this whole outfit that had grown up together, even the white-faced cattle and the fancy horses, seemed to share concern for some dreadful event that might fall upon us. Though the grass along the road was short and the trail was long, surely there was no need to worry about some unknown. Ranching was full of unknowns. Summer range would be good and Montana winter was a long way off. We kept pushing the herd along the trail and toward the mountains of summer range, but still we were uneasy.

We stayed at the Three Forks of the Ruby one day less than usual because the larkspur on the pass and on Poison Creek was so much shorter than in past years. With the hungry cattle we had no choice but to push on to summer range and to hope for grass anywhere.

The old folks were still in the tiny cabin in the middle of nowhere on the pass. The goats were still in the small pasture. Panning gold looked more attractive today than ever before for this ranching family. The kids still peeked from cover as we passed the log house near Centennial Valley, and the big fellow, still wearing heavy woolen underwear and no shirt, stood on the porch. He waved a greeting with his long arms and huge hands, but there was no visit.

The lowest range at summer camp lay almost next to the swamps and the waterlogged meadows of the Centennial Valley. There, finally, we found some feed for the cattle. There was now, for the first time, a showing of new green grass. The cattle spread out here; this new grass would hold them a few days. Then as the grass grew up the slopes, the cattle would follow, until the high ranges came into bloom. We would have summer range yet another year.

We began the trip back to the ranch. The birds, the deer, and the coyotes did not seem to know about the market crash or the poor spring weather. We watched them as we rode along the old pioneer road and on down past the Three Forks and into the Ruby Valley, following the chuck wagon to Silver Spring. Then we left the chuck wagon and rode our horses on toward the ranch at a trot. We opened the gate and led our horses into the barn. Spring range trail was over for one more year.

When the horses and the gear had been cared for and stored away, Father and I headed for the pasture gate. Prince was not there at the gate. The bay mound a few feet away showed the obvious: Prince's ranching days were over; they had ended in the tall sagebrush. We walked slowly over near that favorite horse, he had been dead only a few days. He lay stretched out in a wrinkled heap, he had not struggled in his last moments.

We stood quiet for long moments, and then we saw that Prince's mouth was open. When we looked into his mouth we saw that some of his teeth had grown so long that he could not have eaten the oats in the battered pan. His mouth was lined with gashes along his cheeks and his tongue cut by his long teeth. Prince had starved to death. With all our good intentions we had watched him in those awful last days as the spark of life slowly ebbed away. Heads down, we turned away. No longer did we need to close the pasture gate, or to fill the battered pan with oats. Words did not come but tears made streaks in the dust of the spring trail we had just finished.

It was soon time to get ready for haying, but this year there was no hay to cut, let alone to stack for winter. Wild meadow grass was not six inches tall. Timothy and red top were far from headed. Wild irises were just beginning to bloom, a month late. Only a few of the crimson stars of bird bills showed up in the dampest spots of the meadow. Alfalfa was six inches or so high and far from the purple blooms that meant it was time to cut.

Care was heaped upon the garden. Spuds and garden vegetables, planted late, would have to hurry to make a crop. Apple blossoms had shown just here and there. The seeds of the fruit had long ago been frozen stiff. That was the year that Nature forgot Montana, or at least the headwaters valley.

A month late, we finally began haying. We didn't need much hired help, or any mustangs from the prairie. Only about half the meadows had enough hay to cut. We got one stack of alfalfa instead of several. The garden would have no sweet corn or tomatoes, not even pumpkin for the pie to go with the old strutting gobbler on Thanksgiving Day. There would be no apples, no currants, and very few strawberries for ice cream or preserves. Buffalo berries and chokecherries were not to be found; wild fruit would not bear this year.

Sometimes it seemed that Nature and Montana had come to terms. Yet in the early afternoons the sun beat down unmercifully; the temperature rose, and sweat poured from man and beast. Black clouds rolled and lightning flashed closer and closer, and we unhooked the teams for fear of runaways. Lightning and thunder all came together; the flashes were blinding. Lightning hit trees and fences, and when it hit the swamps, water and mud flew high in the air, like geysers. After the flashes and crashes the rain came—just enough water to shut us down for the day. The almost daily splash of rain and the hot sun drew the substance out of hay we needed so desperately.

One afternoon the air grew still and very hot and heavy. It felt like the steam near a hot spring. The sky began to fill with great blacks clouds, which rolled and swirled about. The light faded and soon daylight almost turned to the dark of night. The mountains faded completely away. I turned the team loose and headed for the nearest brush. In minutes rain hit in a few big drops, driven by a gale so hard they flew almost horizontally.

Across the meadow in a strip most of a hundred yards wide, all that could be seen was the frost of winter, yet this was summertime. The narrow white strip could be seen clear across the valley and the swamps. For the first time since the fences had been built, the posts and the barbed wire stood out clearly in the swamps of cattails and reeds. An occasional snowball— almost three inches across—lay about. It was really a hard hailstone, which fortunately hit no one. The swath of the storm had barely missed all of us in the hayfield, but it could still be seen across the valley and up the slopes of Old Baldy.

In the evening I rode horseback up the road to see the storm's path. The cottonwood trees, the apples trees, and a huge lilac bush at the old Jones homestead had been stripped bare. Limbs, branches, and leaves lay everywhere; most were covered with mud. In the swath of the storm it looked like winter. Late in September the leaves returned and the lilac bush and the apple trees bloomed. I had to wonder what Nature had in store for the headwaters valley of Montana.

a new kind of ranching

Summer range was short and yet the cattle were fat. Traveling home we stayed at the same camps, but we were more than careful of those cattle we knew must be sold. We eased the trail herd along, for we knew the ones to be sold would not bring even a nickel a pound no matter how good they were. Every pound of beef was precious. With luck we could sell down the herd and still have enough cows for another year. River Ranch next year would not likely be the dream of the Frenchman, my grandfather.

We bought some Holstein cows for five dollars each. Milk and cream were a sure way to get cash money. They could be traded for groceries and to the dentist or the doctor if someone happened to get banged up by one of the fancy horses. Three and a half dollars for five gallons of cream was not a fast way to get rich. Putting him to work on that old fifty-gallon churn was a sad way to treat a cowboy. For that job he didn't even need his high-heeled boots, but then, there was no trail dust either.

I took butter to the store one day. A farm lady came in with butter, too. She said, "You know this butter is perfectly all right, but a mouse fell into the churn. Of course, I got him out right away. I would like to trade for a pound of someone else's butter." The storekeeper took the butter to the back of the store and soon returned with a pound of wrapped butter. When the lady had gone out he said, "That lady will find her own butter tastes just as good as yours."

We fixed up the beaver traps and the muskrat traps. I stayed at Grandmother's house in town and sold subscriptions to the *Saturday Evening Post* to get the prize: a knife to skin the beaver we hoped to catch. There was an even greater prize, now that I looked back.

The *Post* was graced with Norman Rockwell's cover pictures, so perfect for the time. Then there were the Caterpillar stories, "Dear Sir" letters to possible customers who might buy one of the newfangled crawler tractors. And the *Post* had national and world news articles and continued stories that would leave one looking forward to the next issue. Best of all, since I was selling the *Post*, it was sent free and post paid. Now I had a magazine to read as well as the pulp Western stories the cowboys left in the bunkhouse.

The Western stories were fun to read, especially in the deep winter. You always knew that the gorgeous girl would be saved and the handsome cowboy would blush like the sun in a Montana blizzard when she kissed him. Then that handsome cowboy would put his two Colt .44s in their holsters, hung low on his hips on the cartridge belt full of shiny brass bullets. He would mount the fiery steed with the bald face and the nervous feet, and with that beautiful damsel nicely seated in front of the saddle he would take up the reins and ride off into the sunset.

The *Post* stories were not so simple as the Westerns, especially those that were continued. Now and then came a real mystery, a bad man with a scowl and a black plug hat and a pocket that bulged with a black pistol and a blackjack. A cowboy's Colt .44 looked like a couple of shotguns alongside the bad man's black pistol. *Post* stories were also about the speakeasies in a dingy neighborhood on some second floor or down a narrow stair in a basement. Speakeasies were not like Walker's Bar in Butte, right on Main Street with the swinging doors in front. The flappers of speakeasy days had slicked-back, all-black hair and short dresses, which led one to think their knobby knees would knock while they waited for the heavy door with the peephole to open. The men in the stories all wore black hats with narrow brims, black suits, and black ties. They smoked big cigars and tailor-made cigarettes. Some of the flappers smoked tailor-mades, too, stuck into a long holder that looked like a cattail stem on fire.

The state required permits for all beaver caught. We had no money for permits, and for little else either. Politicians saved the day. They didn't require permits, and they paid higher prices than the legitimate fur buyers.

The large, old beavers were difficult to catch in the clear creek: They were smart enough to spring the traps with sticks. The young ones were a different proposition, though, so we helped a trapper friend of ours catch a matched set of the small beavers, enough for a full-length fur coat.

Jerre Murphy had planned a surprise for his wife, and although that famous old-time Butte, Montana, sheriff did not know it, we had a surprise planned for him, too. When all the matched kit beavers had been caught and put together they were beautiful to behold. Our friend the trapper was soon on the way to Butte for his meeting with the famous sheriff and hopefully to get his hands on some cash. The sheriff was delighted, complimenting the trapper over and over on the skins that would make his wife the most beautiful fur coat in all of Montana. Jerre Murphy counted out the money, and then he suddenly stopped and exclaimed, "Boys, where is the permit?"

"Sheriff, you never said anything about a permit; you just said, 'Get me a set of those matched beaver skins.' The permit is your problem."

The cash was divided and the hard times were forgotten for a while. Jerre Murphy worked out the permit and his wife got the coat.

We caught a big old beaver in a trap set at a beaver slide on the riverbank just below the hill near the ranch house. Somehow the beaver managed to get the weight off the trap chain that was meant to drown him. He plunged into the river the minute he saw us, but he couldn't reach the trap chain in the river. Father stripped off his warm clothes, jumped into the river, and grabbed the end of the chain. On the road along the big hill, an old car stopped. The horn blew and the folks inside the car came out and waved and shouted. Not having a permit, with those hot traps, I just ran for cover in the brush. Father would have to take care of himself. He froze out of the river real quick, but he never let go of the trap chain. We dispatched the beaver in the cover of the brush, and Father got back into his warm clothes. When we got home there was the old car and those waving people. They were the trappers we had joined to get Jerre Murphy the fur coat. It was a happy event and Father enjoyed it most of all, though he did some considerable shivering.

I was dispatched to get the beaver we left in the brush. I took Old Buster, the all-purpose horse, who did not like cows but might like beavers. The beaver was big and heavy. I found him in the birch and finally got Buster under the beaver. Buster was most unhappy. He ran away, but since he was headed for home that was not so bad.

Dark nights and 3:00 A.M. rising to check traps was worse than any cattle trail or an old cow's bawl at daylight. I could hardly wait for spring trail.

the struggle

Fall and winter saw the country standing still. There was no money and no markets and no work for the unemployed. Investors in the stock market were jumping out of skyscraper windows. Our valley was a barter society; there was no cash. With past years of uncertain and poor weather, and without markets for our livestock, we ranchers were all on the ropes. Any news, even good news sometimes, was frightening. We were afraid to go to town and hear the tales of woe.

Only one bank in the valley went bust, and fortunately it had little investment in the community or the farms and ranches. After the bank holiday all banks in the valley reopened—a return of confidence for everyone. Money, serious though it was to ranchers, was only one of the big problems. The weather changes were just as drastic. Ranching was undergoing a basic change that would forever alter its historic character.

While sitting in the lobby of the bank at Dillon, we were talking to the banker when a truly old-time Montana rancher entered the bank. He wore bib overalls with almost as many patches as original cloth. His shirt was sweat-stained and tobacco juice stained his teeth and left little rivers to his chin. His shoes were in tatters and the soles clapped to the uppers as he approached. He literally fell into a chair.

We all waited quietly as he searched his pockets for another chaw of tobacco. The banker asked, "What happened, Carl?" This was mid-May and summer was close at hand.

"Well, in that snowstorm last week, I lost my sheep. Otto Shulz and I haven't been home yet. I guess we don't have a home anymore."

"How many sheep did you have, and how many do you have left?"

"How do I know? I never bothered to count sheep as long as I have been in the sheep business. I probably lost half, maybe two, three thousand," the rancher replied.

"What do you plan to do and when?" the banker asked.

"Buy some more sheep, of course."

"What do you have for collateral?"

"What's that? I never thought I had to sign anything but my name. That's all I ever done for the last thirty, forty years."

It was pin-drop quiet and the tick-tock of the clock on the wall nearby was loud and clear. "Well, Carl, you buy the sheep," the banker said at last. "I'll pay the checks when they come in and when you get the sheep you need, come on in the bank and we'll work something out." Montana was still Montana, we had not lost it yet. That man's word was all the collateral he needed, though he didn't even know what the word meant.

Banking in Montana continued to be more lenient than in these days. In the thirties, when I was sixteen years old, the banker loaned me $1,600 on my own note, without cosigners. The note was not dated, nor were the amounts filled in. Checks were written on the account as overdrafts without fee. Amounts got filled in if the bank examiner came, or in the fall. There was no interest. What a neat arrangement for a young fellow with his own cattle and a few slick mustangs for trading stock.

Farmers' crops were not producing the yields of the virgin soils of long ago. That, along with the lack of markets and the low prices, was forcing a change to a different kind of crop. Now crops required the expense of fertilizer and added cultivation, along with special types of seeds. The rapid shift from horse power to gasoline power was changing both the farm and ranch industries from top to bottom. The added cost of expensive and complicated machinery was forcing small farms and ranches out of business.

Many farms were simply abandoned; some were consolidated into larger units. The family farm or ranch, with a few cows or sheep, Mom and Pop and a bunch of children, a big garden, and no labor cost, was doomed.

A blizzard that knew no reason, a blizzard of paper and law, descended upon cattle ranching and the once open range.

Sheep and cattle outfits had been an unusual mixture of private property, public land, water holes, and free range. Many of the big outfits with thousands of animals farmed no more than we did—alfalfa hay for a few cows and calves, and oats for the remuda. They ranged over thousands of square miles with an ownership of less than 10 percent of the land. Historic use of land was especially important to these outfits, and it was all based on jawbone—a man's word, which was worth something then—and ownership of water holes.

The good old days were coming to an end, even for those who owned the water holes. Free range for livestock was one thing no rancher could afford to lose; free land was no longer free. Land had value and now the value was recognized. Whoever owned land, be it private, railroad, or public, now demanded payment for its use.

Ranchers who needed grazing land were casting glances at grass anywhere. In years before, ranchers proved up homesteads on public lands, concentrating on the water holes or where the homesteaders would control access to other land. It was no longer legal to homestead public land. Few outfits, even the big outfits, had the means to gain ownership of land needed to run their outfits.

Historically, ranchers financed their operations using livestock as collateral, but debt structures could no longer be serviced on that basis. Old-time ranching meant playing the market. Livestock was a cash asset to which value could readily be assigned, and land was a bill of expense that required expense to maintain and was almost a frozen asset. Most large blocks of rangeland were intertwined with public land or railroad land. No one knew what kind of arrangements would now be required to use those lands.

Financing, a requirement of the changing times, meant disaster for many old-time outfits. Inclement weather, land problems, short grass, and loss of range was putting old-time ranching in handcuffs. Each player had a hand, but he was short some of the cards, the deck was stacked, and the joker was wild. Time alone would tell.

Ranchers had run their outfits out of their hip pockets. Many of them were so short of schooling they, like Grandfather Perrault, could neither read nor write. Their mark was their signature. But many of them were astute and successful businessmen, like Grandfather. Their knowledge of both the wild and domestic animals was legion. Deals these folks made were often for large sums of money. Contracts and agreements were cemented with a shake of the hand. Verbal agreements and commitments were beyond question, their honor and their integrity beyond reproach.

After the bank holiday, financing and operating changed drastically. Associations were set up specifically to finance agriculture. Banks were sold or taken over by stronger banks or by holding companies, whose business was numbers on a sheet of paper that spelled collateral.

Up to then, most all sales were for even cents and dollars, but now the market slipped into decimals. Many old-time ranchers, no matter how short of schooling, could handle the old types of transactions faster than the newfangled adding machines. But the decimals were a different story that reflected upon schooling and not on ability.

For the first time since ranching began, the old-time ranchers were forced to count their stock. Some had no facilities to do so. In the past ranchers had only addressed themselves to herd improvements and to building outfits that fit the land they owned and the free land they used.

In the fall, after the ranch bills were paid, the bank satisfied, and all other obligations cleared, these fellows could only reach into their hip pockets and hope there would be a few bills left.

To the new bankers—many of whom were easterners—the old-time way of doing business was shocking. Neglecting to count a few hundred sheep or cattle simply could not be imagined, let alone accepted. Ranch savvy was no longer relevant. It took most of a lifetime to put a ranching spread together, but a history of success didn't matter anymore. The bottom line was money, and there was no money anywhere—and very little green grass, either.

Owners of some of the best outfits were well up in years, as was my father; his father was now gone. Wills to bequeath the bonanzas, estates, and livestock left lawyers and children competing for control and for the green paper, much like the competition for golden flakes of Alder Gulch. Montana had not lost the flavor of the gold rush days. The age-old pleasures of the flesh often became the work ethic of lucky heirs. They could flash a roll of folding money, but took little interest in the cattle brand that made it.

sorrowful days

The mountains and the gulches were crawling with prospectors and miners, as creeks were again being panned for the
yellow metal. Local merchants were more likely to grubstake
the simple and inexpensive needs of a lone miner than the
costly credit of ranchers. Every so often one of the grubstakes
would pay off. Gold fever is as old as man himself. There were
some small mines working. The miners spent their pay in the
valley and they ate some of our cream and butter. This was the
only cash crop in the valley and it was a gift from heaven,
even if it was not green grass.

There were all kinds of mine promoters. The most daring
one built a bridge across the river to get to a mine. Then he
built a mill to process ore not yet found, and drove a tunnel a
couple hundred feet into Table Mountain. He paid good wages
and all his bills and P. K. Wriggley kept sending the cash.

Chewing gum was very popular in the Ruby Valley. At
twenty dollars an ounce, gold in those days would buy a lot of
chewing if you did not use tobacco.

Our printed page was the *Madisonian*, the local newspaper,
and the *Montana Standard*, the newspaper of the Anaconda
Mining Company, which actually ran Montana. The
Standard's headlines were in bold letters; articles praised the
company and told dreary tales of the Great Depression. All
the news was company slanted, telling of the need to lay off
more miners, disparaging the miners' strike votes, and
describing the company's challenges of strike-breaking and
scab labor. The glowing editorials of the deeds and prowess of
the company in the legislature left little doubt of Doc Heller's
observation: Pass two bills, one to go home and one to mind
your own business.

That year we went to Butte with the county agent to get some chemicals for grasshopper control, although the cold weather had left little problem in our area. We had enough grasshoppers for fish bait, but not enough to ruin the garden or eat up the wagon tongues and harness.

When we got to Fish Creek bench, the Milwaukee train was stopped on the hill west of the road. We stopped to find out the reason the train stood still. When we got out of the car, grasshoppers were flying in huge clouds above us. Those big gluttons dropped from the clouds and the ground seemed to crawl with a sea of bugs. The train crew was all around the engines looking at the tracks, plainly confused. So many grasshoppers had been crushed upon the tracks that the driver wheels of the engine would only turn and spin on the slick rails.

Some of the train's car doors were open, and we could see whole families inside: men, women, and children and some small babies. From our small world, a community we could all relate to and manage to provide for, none of us were prepared for this heartwrenching sight. Why would more than a hundred people be in those boxcars on a train headed for Butte, Montana? What possibly, in that already strife-torn town, a one-company and a one-union town, could these people find but more hardship, hunger, and privation?

Silently we went on to Butte, loaded the chemicals, and then went on uptown to one of the best restaurants. No longer was this restaurant shiny and spotless, no longer did the waitresses have little lace-trimmed aprons, white blouses, and black skirts. This was just any old restaurant now. There was room for perhaps a hundred patrons, yet we were the only ones in the dining room for lunch.

Prohibition was still a joke. Walker's Bar still had sawdust on the floor, but only a few customers. Street corners were crowded with miners with the deep, hacking, gasping, and spitting coughs of miners' con. Few of the fellows displayed a smile, and there was little conversation.

Almost all of the mines that before were so active, and that we watched intently as the great head frame wheels turned and the cables moved over them, were silent. We walked back to the car and headed for home. When we got to the Fish Creek bench it was almost dark, and we were all relieved to see that the train was gone. We were fortunate, but the fate of the homeless people on that almost empty train filled our thoughts for days.

With the warm days of summer, folks who no longer had a home or any special place to go, like those on the train, would hike along the country roads. Every day someone stopped and inquired about something to do to earn a meal or a place to sleep. From the professional hobo to the city slicker to the failed farmer, rancher, or businessman, folks of all stripes crossed the ranch house threshold. This was an experience never before encountered in the remote Montana valley. Nevertheless, that year I didn't have to chop or stack any wood for the Home Comfort stove. I never had to clean the barn or hoe the garden. The hobos, ranchers, and farmers down on their luck saw that the work was done. Often they would work until late in the afternoon and then they would wearily walk along the country road, hoping to find another stopping place and something to eat. As we watched these poor folks trudge along the road, heads down, our hearts were heavy with their misfortunes.

One day, a man well up in years stopped at the house. His threadbare business suit had once been neat and fashionable. His homburg hat led one to speculate that this fellow had once really been somebody. As he ate along with all of us he spread his handkerchief upon his lap. He obviously once enjoyed a gracious home and life. He didn't look at the woodpile, and he had most likely never seen or thought about a garden, a barn, or even a ranch. This old fellow had to be a city businessman.

When he finished eating, he looked around the table. First at Mother, who cooked the most bountiful meal he had eaten in days, then at Father, and then at the other passers-by who also wore threadbare clothes. Ashamed and deeply moved by his own plight, he hung his head and clasped the handkerchief upon his lap. Tears fell from his eyes onto the empty plate before him. Slowly he got up from the table, but he did not speak.

Wearily he trod to the door as tears streamed down his tired and forlorn face. The old man stopped and gazed at the yard gate that opened to the country road. With eyes turned to the ground he stepped ever so slowly through the gate and along the path to the rutty road that led to nowhere.

barbed wire

Spring saw barbed wire on the prairie. The south end, before the Ruby Mountains, was fenced by a sheep man with three strands of barbed wire. The cattle were fenced out and the sheep were free to go where they pleased. The jawbone agreements of the users of the prairie no longer meant a thing.

There was no longer water near the timber for cattle—the river had been fenced out years earlier. Now the wild mustangs traveled most of ten miles to water at the north end of the prairie. Their hooves cut roads across the sod. The snowbanks of winter barely sustained those horses until the ditch at the north edge of the prairie ran full of water.

The wild horses had become so degenerate and they were so starved that some of the old ones had feet as big as a washtub. It would be easy to run the old studs down with a Shetland pony. No one cared who owned any of those horses, not even the ones that had a brand and, at one time, an owner. Some of those owners had been ruined by the hard times, and some had for one reason or another deserted the Ruby Valley. There was no pity for these poor animals, who often died from the combination of little or bad water and starvation in winter storms.

With the mustangs uncontrolled, there were at least three or four hundred of them out on the shrunken prairie range. This range was still mostly public land that had been shared by ranchers since the beginning of livestock raising in the headwaters valley. There used to be a few hundred head of cattle, a band or two of sheep, and a few wild horses on the prairie. Now there was only a small bit of prairie left to support hundreds of horses, the same sheep, a few cattle—and miles of barbed wire.

Grass was now so short it barely covered the feet of horses and cattle. Jackrabbits moved near the edge of the prairie, closer to the fields, where they could find something to eat. Anywhere was better than the sorry prairie.

The disbanding of the United States Cavalry was the last straw for the mustangs. Fine stallions with good blood lines were placed on ranches and there was no use for wild horses. Gasoline had taken care of most of the horse-drawn machinery. Wild horses were now only a nuisance.

With great leisure the bands of sheep ranged from the timber to and fro across the prairie, from watering hole to watering hole. In a year or two there would be no prairie—even the prickly pear would be gone.

The prairie must be saved from the sheep and the wild horses or it would be lost for everyone. We watched as those sheep cropped the short grass to the roots and the horses chopped trails to watering holes. As long as there was a spear of grass the sheep would find it, if the horses didn't get there first.

When the prairie became more like a county road than a field of grass, the sheepherder got greedy. We met him on our leased land—the land with a water hole—and were ready to teach a lesson. Several screaming cowboys pushed a couple hundred wild mustangs across the prairie toward his herd of sheep. The herder ran away from his sheep faster than any coyote ran toward a fat lamb. He had a death grip on the string of tin cans he used as a noisemaker, and those cans were clattering to beat the band. He was followed closely by his two dogs as the mustangs hit the band of sheep.

I pulled Smoke up, slowed down to watch, and stopped yelling. The sheepherder had stopped running and became a statue. His face turned ashen white, and his scraggly beard that looked like a browner version of grass on the prairie, blew in the wind. A black hat flopped down over his ears, and nearly covered his wide-open eyes. He stood transfixed with his patched jeans stuffed into high-laced boots. His hand was white from the steel grip he had on that string of cans that now gave not a tinkle. He was flanked on both sides by his dogs, whose ears were erect. The dogs were frozen in place with their tails between their legs. The frightened threesome watched as their mob of sheep was stampeded by wild mustangs.

The sheep were flying through the air, ewes bleating and lambs mewing, all in fear and many in pain. The mustangs were pawing, falling, and racing to get through the milling sheep in their path. I, the young rancher, born and bred to hate sheep, was back to screaming and yelling. "Push those horses, to hell with those sheep, save our grass!" Two hundred stampeding mustangs made a substantial difference in the number of grazing sheep and left food for all the coyotes, hawks, and eagles for the rest of the summer. Our range had been hurt bad, but what was left of the sheep never ventured anywhere near it ever again.

Our summer range, some of which was public land, was also short. The Taylor Grazing Act and the U.S. Forest Service now came into play. There were meetings and letters, and the ranges had quotas and allotments of stock. Any quotas set were likely based on the past use of the range. It was not only a good idea to control the public lands, it was a necessity that came years too late. The weather was poor for so long that there was no good information concerning what the ranges could produce. Native climax grass can take a hundred years to reach its peak. Yet in this last decade these great ranges went into a sort of dormant mode and the yields had shrunk to low levels. Old-time ranchers like Grandfather and Father saw the range at its best, and they practiced good range management. Management of the public lands did nothing but preserve the ranges we depended on.

Many of the improvements on the public lands may be directly credited to the Civilian Conservation Corps of the depression years. When the program ended, some of the city youngsters were western hooked. Some became ranchers, lumbermen, and farmers, and the big city poverty and stress that had sent them here in the first place was lost forever.

a year to remember

There were days of sun and smiles. Spring brought the rain, and the grass began to green and to grow even on the sorry prairie. Meadow flowers followed spring as close as winter followed fall. There was little old grass left; the willow branches were bare and cottonwood trees still had no leaves. With a few more days of sun, though, the little cotton balls we used to fire in our pea shooters in school would begin to form. Soon would come the cotton and the wonderful odor of the cottonwood sap as it flowed up the trunks and into the branches and leaves.

The outfit got together for the spring trail drive. The sun and rain that Nature levied upon her charges would lead once again through the short grass and the bare hillsides to summer range. The usual preparations would be hard, and the excitement was not quite there.

The trail drive began in a rain and snow squall, with heavy hearts. The old, trail-wise cows knew the trail well. Short grass and cold wind drove them like a whip. The few heifers and their tiny calves had trouble keeping up the pace. We were all hoping to find green grass up ahead, yet knowing full well that there was only a slim chance. The calf boot on the chuck wagon was already full.

At the forks of the Ruby, only a few spears of last year's grass dotted the meadows and the hillsides. The cattle were tired and hungry, and the calves footsore. This was a long trail, and footsore calves slowed it down, but the white-faced cows would never leave a calf far behind.

It was a trail to remember. We carefully spread the cattle around the hillsides, hoping they would find grass or other food. The bright green larkspur was very short, but it was still deadly. Somehow, cattle stomachs had to be filled before tackling that deadly patch of bad news.

Finally, the drive was over the rim and on to summer range. Once the herd was past the larkspur, the feed turned for the better and our hopes rose accordingly. On the divide, in bright sunlight, flocks of water birds flew among the ponds and the streams of Centennial Valley. The grim trail turned to joy in the outdoors. It would be a good year after all.

Back home the crops were slow and hay was short. There was no barn dance that Fourth. The fear of fire in the uninsured barn and the large number of valley folks on a stay-alive economy had taken a toll. For entertainment that summer we had to get by on fishing and scouting the mountains for the lost gold mine.

Fall came. Ducks and geese flew south for the winter in wedges. The flocks of prairie chickens were large that year, and the young ones could not be distinguished from the old birds. Beavers and rats were building houses and repairing dams. Willow patches along the creek had many stumps of recently cut shoots that would be winter food for beavers. Swamp reeds had been cut in patches by the muskrats.

The fall drive to the ranch from summer range saw the climax grasses gone to seed and the daisies of the mountains become long stalks with black heads filled with seed for next summer. The trail-wise cows were already dropping down from the ridges and the high mountain swamps and peat bogs. Most of the little ponds and lakes were frozen over, and the creeks had a rim of ice wherever they ran around the bends in the meadows and the current slowed down. The old cows were eyeing the trail to low country and the ranch.

Driving a few hundred cattle was not much trouble when we were used to driving a couple thousand. The herd trailed down the big hill and into the ranch gates and the pastures.

Fall pasture was shorter each year. Year after year of unfavorable weather meant that alkali was beginning to coat meadows and they were beginning to show throughout the whole valley. There would barely be enough hay to get our sick cow outfit through the winter. It was beginning to look like another winter of milking cows, turning the old barrel

Perrault Ranch house

churn, and running a trap line . . . perhaps even pitching hay in forty-below weather every day.

Winter didn't wait long. Instead of Indian summer, October was filled with blustery wind, freezing nights, and lots of blowing snow. One storm followed the next, though there was never enough snow to make more than tiny drifts behind the brush and buildings.

Christmas came and went without a trip to Butte, and without presents. Father found twenty dollars that was misplaced in a cupboard long ago. We used this bonanza to have Christmas dinner with friends and relatives. As I looked around that table filled with good food and loved ones, I thought of the sad faces of the people we saw earlier on the train to Butte, and I was thankful for my good fortune. When Christmas was over, a new feeling of hope filled our hearts as we turned toward the new year.

One afternoon the sky went black and clouds rolled in from the north when we were out hunting jackrabbits along the bench rim. It was January 6, my father's birthday. As soon as we saw the clouds we headed for the ranch house, and within an hour the temperature had dropped more than fifty degrees. Snow was falling almost horizontal, pushed by the wind so hard the flakes hurt my face. At the barn the cows and horses were waiting to get inside. We tied them in the stalls as fast as we could and headed back to the ranch house. Already it was almost a whiteout—when we hit the road between the barn and the house we had to get down on our hands and knees to follow the path on up to the house. Those few feet seemed like miles in the blinding snow and wind.

The two-story ranch house was wood-framed and wood-sided with plastered walls inside. Insulation was unknown or at least not used in those days. The second-story ceiling was boards with felt paper and shingle roofing. This construction stopped most of the wind but little else. The floors were not carpeted, and to walk in bare feet was just like walking on the skating pond. The north windows of the house were frozen stiff with ice so thick that one could not see outside.

Cold kerosene for the lamps poured from the can as thick and white as milk. The thermometer was down near the bottom, forty-five below. There was only one thing to do, though it was early evening: turn the lamps out and go to bed where it was warm. The storm was sure to ease off by morning.

Being in the upstairs room in the ranch house was just the same as being outdoors except that there was no snow blowing around. The feather bed and the down-filled mattress were like ice. I crawled into this cave thinking that with the old buffalo robe on top I would soon be warm and fast asleep. It did not happen quite like that. In a few minutes I was warm, all right, but I had to tell myself that the heavy buffalo robe on top would surely keep me from being blown away as the house shook and leaned in the wind. Surely the roof would blow off. I crawled even farther under the buffalo robe. It was not safe up here in this room. The wind whined and whistled along the eaves and rattled the windows. I knew that in the morning there would be tiny snow drifts inside the room by those windows. The moaning and the lowing of that vicious storm sounded like a cow that was trying to have a calf.

At last I became accustomed to the sounds of the storm, and fell asleep. It was light when I finally awoke—about seven or eight in the morning. I could hear the stir downstairs and wondered how much longer I could wait till the stove got hot. I jumped up, pulled on my clothes and coat, and ran downstairs. Fully dressed and mackinaw-clad, I hurried to the little house in the corner of the yard.

The house still shook and creaked, and the wind still howled. Windows were frozen over with ice half an inch thick. The house had survived the night, and now it looked like it must survive another day of storm. The only difference in the storm today was a little longer pause between the blasts and a bit less snow. Even behind the fence and other barriers there was only a little of the powder-dry snow. It seemed that most of the snow had been blown clear out of Montana by the fierce wind.

We tied binder twine to the dinner bell post and headed for the barn, bumping the corral fence till we found the gate. The two lanterns in the cooler house barely kept the milk from freezing. The storm still raged. This was a Montana ranch caught in a real blizzard, guaranteed to still the strongest heart and pale the toughest skin.

We had not yet begun to feed the cattle, but now the storm decreed that we do so. The storm eased off in the late afternoon and we again did the chores in the gusty cold wind and snow, with the cattle lowing in the field.

In the early morning of the next day, the house no longer creaked and shook, but all the windows were frozen over and we couldn't see outside. The storm had lost its grip, but it was fifty-two below and we couldn't pour the frozen kerosene from its can. Everything was frozen stiff in the bitter cold.

The barn had a pile of snow on its south side most of six feet high. The road into the field was clear, but on the south side along the fence the wild rosebushes were covered with drifts.

Now was the time to start hauling hay for the rest of the winter. The breath of the team made a plume of steam; icicles hung from the horses' faces. The calves who got out of the weaner corral could not be separated that day. To work cattle in that icebox would easily freeze their lungs, and those of the horses, too. Someday we would get them separated, but they would never be weaned.

Cattle bawled and followed the wagon as the hay was pitched out. We trusted the Montana weather, so we filled the wagon again and headed for the ranch house. In the corner of the field, next to a small patch of brush, stood a lone cow. Her head was down, almost touching the ground. She was humped up and still and mute. I looked more closely and saw which cow it was—my pride and joy. As a calf she had been my entry into the cattle business. There on the ranch she was the only off-color critter in the herd. Finally, after having watched her all through the feeding, I suggested we take a look as we were ready to head for home. "No use, son, she is froze," my father said.

I got that roan heifer as a calf and gone into the cow business in a rather unusual way. I had a few dollars from the trap line, and one day my uncle and his friend came to the ranch in a dilapidated old truck, carrying the roan calf. They were trying to raise enough cash so they could spend a few days in the stone house at Virginia City. Seemed they had some hard luck and gotten a few days of vacation for selling some Montana cough syrup in the Prohibition days. It was necessary to get enough money to feed themselves so they could serve their time: At that time, justice meant sleeping in the jail and feeding yourself. The sheriff, of course, got the money for feeding the prisoners as a bonus. All sentences were served, all laws were upheld, at a minimum of inconvenience to everyone. The calf cost me twelve dollars. Now there was a roan cow statue on River Ranch, an ice monument to Montana ranching that would last until the sun of spring.

Each day is yesterday's tomorrow. We woke up to an old black north with rolling clouds of ice and snow. The binder twine was still tied off between the house and the barn, and it was a good thing because often the trail could not be followed in the blinding snow. Each night we went to bed to the howl of the winter wind.

Near mid-January, it finally warmed to ten or so below, and we got the calves back to the corral in which they belonged. Some had to be weaned all over; some would never be weaned. They would be sold.

No one had stopped to visit, or for any other reason, for a long time. The roads were closed to all but horses. It was a good thing that we had a cellar full of vegetables and shelves full of canned goods.

Near February it got warm and quiet enough that we tried to ride to town. Halfway there, the north turned black again, and we barely beat the storm back to the ranch. After a few days of waiting, we tried again and succeeded. The news was all storm. Lots of stock lost, some people frozen, and most farmers and ranchers crawling out of the worst set of storms in memory.

The mail was light, but a sheaf of local papers would fill several evenings. There was sure to be enough cold weather left to read all the news and some more books, too.

One February day when we had finished feeding the cattle, we saw a herd coming toward the ranch. It was cold, about zero, but the wind was quiet and it was clear as I went out to help drive the cattle. A rancher who was out of hay was moving them south to some feed he had purchased.

In the morning after breakfast we saddled up the horses. Father fed our cattle and I helped the rancher along his way. It was cold and hazy in the north, but there was not a breath of wind. We strung the cattle along the road through the snowdrifts. They traveled slowly, and by late afternoon they were impossible to drive.

The sky turned black, and the cattle must have sensed a storm about to fall upon us—many of the cows went into labor. With the first flakes of snow driven by the wind, the first calf dropped. We were on the edge of the prairie, with no shelter and in the midst of a blizzard. The storm hurried Nature up to get the calves born right away. We pulled off the saddles and used our saddle blankets to try to dry the little calves.

The cattle were bunched up close to each other with their backs to the storm. We could only see the cows near us, and it was getting bitter cold. Near the middle of the night the snow and wind eased off. The cold settled in with a vengeance all its own.

When daylight came, we saw that we were near shelter and hay. We pushed what was left of the herd through the gate to the safety of the brush shelter. Bareback, we rode back to where the storm hit to check on the calves and to find our saddles and blankets. It was very cold, but the sky was clear, and the storm had passed. The little mounds, red hide and white drift on the lee side, needed no explanation. Some of the mounds were still guarded by cows unwilling to give up their newborns to death. Some of the mounds were bigger and had no one to guard them.

On the edge of the prairie I found my saddle, but I was saddened and confused. The blanket was not worth looking for, at least not today. I threw the saddle on Smoke and slowly we walked toward home.

With Smoke in the barn, I trudged on up to the house. It was fifty-two below. In just one day, that blizzard had destroyed those fine cattle and broken a rancher. There was no need to talk about his fate or his fortune. No words were needed that February morning; we were all worn out. I fought all night to help the rancher save his outfit, and for nothing. Father and Mother were with two newborn calves in front of the Home Comfort range. Their many years on this very old River Ranch told the real story of this winter disaster.

Our thoughts were all the same, though no one said a word. Would our turn be next?

indian summer

A March chinook came early and water flowed from the snow-banks in streams. Fields were frozen dry because of the limited snow cover during winter. Chinook water flowed over them and just thawed the ice. The snow was gone from the mountains. Spring rain or snow would have to save the crops because the soil was dry when the wind stopped.

April sat on her hands but somehow managed to stop the wind. May was unusually hot, and what rain there was fell with great bluster in a few large drops. May rain barely kept the dust down. It was near midyear, but the spring range looked like midwinter. The old days of twenty-five days of rain in June no longer could be taken for granted. What a blessing rain like that would have been, but it never came.

There were no sheep on the prairie. The fence that kept the cattle away from the mountains and allowed the sheep to go where they pleased was no longer needed. The profits for sheep disappeared and economics did what no one else could do: drove the sheep from the prairie grass.

The county held horse roundups to control the wild horse herds. Roundups, first on one range and then on another, could be profitable. Branded horses could be redeemed for a small fee or sold. Others, not branded, could be purchased for almost nothing. Horses not sold or redeemed were sent to the packing house. They ended up in Europe in tin cans.

High water forgot to come that unusual year. The rivers never ran bank full. Some of the meadow bogs were almost dry, yet dry weather was supposed to be a month in the future. Meadows were white, with alkali. Spring flowers that always covered the meadows were now just small patches in the damp spots. Timothy and red top were a scant few inches high.

We shared what was left of the prairie spring range with our neighbor ranchers. We went to summer range weeks late, knowing the range would still be too short. We moseyed up the trail looking for grass anywhere, counting the days and wishing for rain and sun to make plants grow.

When the cloudburst came with clouds as black as night, flashes of lightning, and crashes of thunder, all at once it seemed like a river had moved next to the bunkhouse. A flood of water raced down the gravel wash, past the open bunkhouse door, and toward the prairie. The flood was a soup of water, sand, and gravel, and even some rocks. It was so composed that it barely flattened out at the banks of the wash.

The drenching rain stopped and the sky cleared as quickly as it had clouded. The air was heavy with warm moisture. As I walked to the house from the bunkhouse I noticed that every depression was filled with warm water. The whole yard was a hopping, jumping pool full of tiny green frogs. By nightfall the yard along the prairie bench was again dry, the little green frogs were gone.

The cloudburst flowed down the gravel wash and washed out the old pioneer ditch close to the cottonwood trees. The ditch was now a pile of gravel and stones where the flood had passed. I was driving the team on the slip as we cleared the ditch. The slip was turned around and the team was standing still as we worked with shovels in the ditch. I went over to sit on the upturned slip. Suddenly there was a *bzzz* sound, and only my grip on the ends of the lines stopped my backward flight through the air. Between the handles of that old-fashioned slip, all coiled up, was a big green rattler. He had ridden the cloudburst down from the prairie to the ditch, and now that I had my wits back, he was on the way to rattlesnake heaven.

When the haying began—with what little hay there was— surveyors could be seen measuring the ditches, measuring the river and creek flows, and calculating the areas of cultivated and watered lands. A dam for irrigation would be built on the river near the gate at the old toll road, where the river flowed into the valley. This dam would hold water to irrigate thousands of acres of prairie.

Once the dam was built, the whole natural sequence of high water, flooded meadows, and weather patterns would be drastically altered. All the wild meadows along the river basin would be changed forever. Never again would there be high water to scour the meadows and then to coat them with the river silt that made them so productive. Each of the last few years of dry weather and the failed spring floods left the meadows like a sick man. The once thick cover of the climax grasses of Grandfather's day would now be condemned to alkali bogs. The backbone of this ranch would also be gone— the meadows and the spring range of the prairie would be companions of lost natural crops. The ranch fields along the bench could still be planted to regular farm crops. The soil was fertile and the yields would not be affected because there was never a shortage of irrigating water for those fields.

During the final years of 1880, ranching—ranging herds of cattle on the plains of grass—was well established in Montana. Agriculture was then favorably competing with mining as the most important industry. But the terrible storms of the late 1880s wiped out the cattle industry in the open plains.

Grandfather Perrault was here in the Stinkingwater Valley in those years. His cattle were the lucky ones in the protected headwaters of the Missouri River. Here in this valley, that winter had been just another Montana winter. The spring and summer of that winter saw Nature levy her might upon all of the outdoors in Montana. Forest fires and prairie fires raged everywhere. Even the mines shut down to fight the fires. When the fires finally died out most of the prairie grass was gone and forests were sorely scorched. Livestock went to market by the trainload in summer instead of fall. Ranchers had to start over and rebuild the herds and their outfits.

Bad as the 1880s were, 1919 saw failed crops far worse than any known time in this valley of the Ruby. There were cases of starved stock because no feed could be sent to the valley. Farmers failed because no crops would bloom, even when irrigated. Crops in the valley were like those the nesters had on the prairie: almost nonexistent.

The year 1929 is known for the great market crash. That crash somehow brought along the most unfavorable weather for ranch and farm ever seen in Montana, and it was still there years later. By the end of the summer of 1937 it was clear that the weather was not paying attention to the times and would likely settle in for a long stay of more bad news. That kind of weather had by that time worn out its welcome.

It was sure, as we packed the gear and the chuck wagon at summer range for another trip back to the ranch, that ranching in the headwaters was again at a crossroads. As we followed the trail out of the Centennial Valley to the ranch, we wondered if the hard times of the 1880s, 1919, and 1929 were settling in forever.

On the trail to the ranch from summer range we were filled with trepidation. We knew there was no market and almost no cattle buyers. The knowledge that the fall pasture would not be there was a heavy worry. As we trailed along other ranchers came by, lamenting the same conditions. A decision for the fall sale had to be made, and soon. The steers, the dry cows, and even some of the producing herd had to be sold.

When we reached the ranch, all the ranchers with cattle in the herd decided to pool the cattle to be sold and shipped to Los Angeles, California. All the steers and the others to be sold were cut out the last day along the trail.

Melrose, Montana, is a small village about eighteen miles west of River Ranch, on the banks of the Big Hole River. It was a station on the Union Pacific Railroad. Melrose was also famous for the big trout that swam in the river nearby. We trailed the cattle to the little village and into the stockyards to be shipped by train to Los Angeles.

The engine spotted the cattle cars and they were soon filled and ready to roll. As the last car pulled out of the station and rolled down the mainline, I looked at Father and the other Montana cattlemen. Tears streaked down his cheeks and washed away the trail dust, the alkali, and the storms of Montana ranching.

It was a new day. The hour was barely past dawn at River Ranch, and the sky was clear blue. The corral had a white skirt of frost along the poles, and the bolt heads of the braces were like little white hats. The horseshoe latch was cold to the bare hand. The water trough had a skim of ice near the plank edges. Smoke was getting old, and his hide, which was once dark gray, had turned much lighter in color. Frost showed only along his backbone in those tan and roan Appaloosa spots.

The white-faced cow across the dust of the corral had a back of shiny white frost crystals—Nature's way of telling us that soon enough winter would be on the way. The corral dust was inches deep from years of use. Many years had passed since those corral posts were planted.

The posts leaned a bit here and there. The poles between the posts were scarred by many kicks from wild mustangs, and some sagged as a result. Some of the top poles were scarred where those mustangs had clawed to get over and back out on the prairie. Some poles had teethmarks to go along with the marks of vicious kicks. There were long dried splotches of blood along some of the poles where some mustang hit a knot or a rough spot as he raced around the corral, desperately looking for a way back out to his prairie home or trying to dodge some cowboy's rope.

The snub post in the middle of the corral had only a sliver of bark here and there. The hard-twist rope burns were neat bands along that post. Many times some cowboy had raced for that post as his lariat went snug about the front feet of one of those mustangs racing around the corral. Once tied off to the snub post, it would be only seconds till that mustang lay help-less in the corral with a cowboy's knee on his throat and his nose held in the air. Then the hot iron would sometimes make his hide smoke, and he would no longer be free. Sometimes he lost his status in the wild herd as he lay there helpless in the dirt and the sharp knife ended one career.

The log water trough was full that morning with a tiny skim of ice. There was a lot more water in it than there had been the time Smoke deposited a cowboy in there one frosty morning a year or so ago. Smoke's thigh had a slice of white across it where the hard twist had sung along that hip. Hard-twist rope tied to some wild cow left marks like that on the saddle horns, too.

The sound of bawling cows could not be heard today. The oat can rattled gently and Smoke's ears twitched most every which way. They missed no sound. His one white eye had seen it all and the other eye was casing that old, beat-up pan of oats near the water trough. The flowing muscles of his powerful legs moved ever so slightly as though he were going to jump the fence. Those muscles needed only to flex a bit as his head dropped to taste the candy in the pan.

The little fall calf, with the pink nose and the white scrubbed-clean face, stood as close as possible to her mother, the white-faced cow in the corral. She turned her head first this way and then that. Her eyes surveyed, with great distrust, Smoke and me and the pole corral that held those almost-wild critters. Oats meant nothing to that cow, and she was not thirsty. She was wondering how she got into this sorry place so far from the outdoors that was her world. Her one thought was that little calf. She twisted her head about, watching Smoke, on full alert.

Smoke, the progeny of a circus horse, lifted his head and watched the cow and her calf as he carefully munched oats. Smoke, that almost-wild cow, and others like him would always be the players in this great space of sun, storm, grass, and Nature. Cowboys would be here with them, too. There would be another year that would bring grass, green and lush again. The great mountain meadows would be bountiful, and our cows, the fine, white-faced Herefords—the progeny of the calico beginners that Grandfather and Father nurtured those many years—would be here, too, and they would be content.

River Ranch was a cow outfit and cow outfits can only see the future—they forget the past.